THE NO-COOK COOKBOOK

RECIPES BY
REBECCA WOOLLARD

DK

Author Rebecca Woollard

Editor Katie Lawrence
Project art editor Charlotte Bull
Designer Charlotte Jennings
Food stylist and home economist Denise Smart
Photographer Ruth Jenkinson
Recipe tester Jessica Meyer
Production editor Dragana Puvacic
Senior production controller Ena Matagic
Jacket designer Charlotte Bull
Jacket co-ordinator Issy Walsh
Managing editor Jonathan Melmoth
Managing art editor Diane Peyton Jones
Publishing manager Francesca Young
Creative director Helen Senior
Publishing director Sarah Larter

First published in Great Britain in 2021 by
Dorling Kindersley Limited
DK, One Embassy Gardens, 8 Viaduct Gardens,
London, SW11 7BW

This book was made with Forest Stewardship
Council ™ certified paper – one small step
in DK's commitment to a sustainable future.

For more information go to
www.dk.com/our-green-pledge

FSC
www.fsc.org
MIX
Paper from
responsible sources
FSC™ C018179

CONTENTS

HOW THE BOOK WORKS

This cookbook will help you to become more independent in the kitchen. It's packed full of delicious meals, top tips for storage, and instructions for how to grow your own fruit and vegetables.

"Tip" suggestions help you make a recipe, or tell you how to store the finished creation.

RECIPES

Follow the recipe steps to learn how to whip up each and every dish in this cookbook.

This is the list of ingredients you'll need for a recipe.

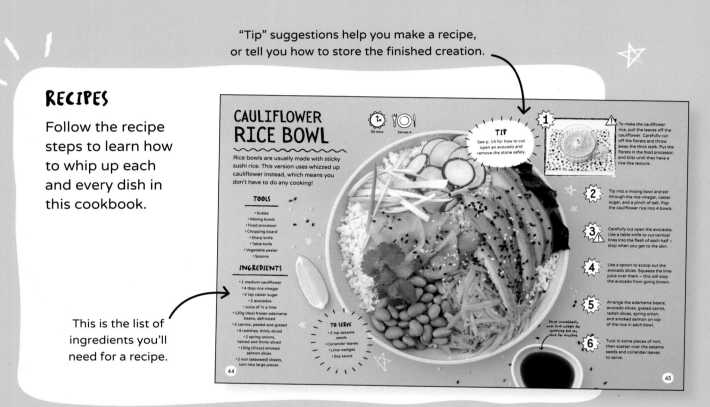

RECIPE VARIATIONS

Some pages have different types of the same recipe on them.

Look out for "Change it up!" circles – they'll tell you extra ways to make a recipe.

FOLLOW-ON RECIPES

The recipes on these pages follow on from the previous page. They show you even more suggestions for different recipe variations.

Each recipe is broken down into steps.

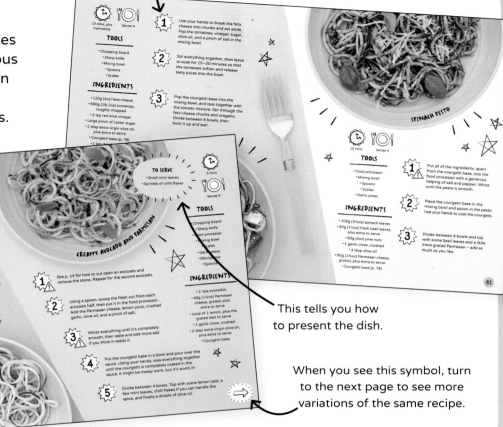

10 mins, plus marinating · Serves 4

TOOLS
- Chopping board
- Sharp knife
- Mixing bowl
- Spoons
- Scales

INGREDIENTS
- 120g (4oz) feta cheese
- 500g (1lb 2oz) tomatoes, roughly chopped
- 2 tsp red wine vinegar
- Large pinch of caster sugar
- 2 tbsp extra virgin olive oil, plus extra to serve
- Courgetti base (p. 78)
- 1 tsp chilli

1. Use your hands to break the feta cheese into chunks and set aside. Pop the tomatoes, vinegar, sugar, olive oil, and a pinch of salt in the mixing bowl.

2. Stir everything together, then leave to soak for 15–20 minutes so that the tomatoes soften and release tasty juices into the bowl.

3. Pop the courgetti base into the mixing bowl, and toss together with the tomato mixture. Stir through the feta cheese chunks and oregano. Divide between 4 bowls, then twist it up and eat!

SPINACH PESTO

10 mins · Serves 4

TOOLS
- Food processor
- Mixing bowl
- Spoons
- Scales
- Garlic press

INGREDIENTS
- 100g (3½oz) spinach leaves
- 40g (1½oz) fresh basil leaves, plus extra to serve
- 60g (2oz) pine nuts
- 1 garlic clove, crushed
- 3 tbsp extra virgin olive oil
- 50g (1¾oz) Parmesan cheese, grated, plus extra to serve
- Courgetti base (p. 78)

1. Put all of the ingredients, apart from the courgetti base, into the food processor with a generous helping of salt and pepper. Whizz until the pesto is smooth.

2. Place the courgetti base in the mixing bowl and spoon in the pesto. Use your hands to coat the courgetti.

3. Divide between 4 bowls and top with some basil leaves and a little more grated Parmesan – add as much as you like.

81

COURGETTI

Using a spiralizer will give you courgette strands that look very similar to spaghetti. But unlike spaghetti, courgetti doesn't need to be cooked – just add a tasty sauce and enjoy a healthy dinner.

20 mins · Serves 4

TOOLS
- Chopping board
- Sharp knife
- Spiralizer
- Scissors

FOR THE COURGETTI BASE
- 4 courgettes, halved with bases trimmed

1. See p. 14 for how to use a spiralizer. Use it to cut the courgette – you should end up with a big tangle of courgetti. Repeat for the remaining courgettes.

2. If the strands are longer than normal spaghetti, use scissors to trim them down. Use the courgetti as soon as you've spiralized it – it doesn't keep very well and can become soft.

3. Choose one of the three sauces on this page or the next, coat the courgetti, twirl it around your fork, and enjoy!

CHANGE IT UP!
If you don't have a spiralizer, a julienne peeler is a great alternative, and will produce lovely courgette strands.

78

TO SERVE
- Small mint leaves
- Sprinkle of chilli flakes

CREAMY AVOCADO AND PARMESAN

5 mins · Serves 4

TOOLS
- Chopping board
- Sharp knife
- Food processor
- Mixing bowl
- Scales
- Garlic press
- Microplane
- Spoons

INGREDIENTS
- 2 ripe avocados
- 40g (1½oz) Parmesan cheese, grated, plus extra to serve
- Juice of 1 lemon, plus the grated zest to serve
- 1 garlic clove, crushed
- 2 tbsp extra virgin olive oil, plus extra to serve
- Courgetti base

1. See p. 14 for how to cut open an avocado and remove the stone. Repeat for the second avocado.

2. Using a spoon, scoop the flesh out from each avocado half, then put it in the food processor. Add the Parmesan cheese, lemon juice, crushed garlic, olive oil, and a pinch of salt.

3. Whizz everything until it's completely smooth, then taste and add more salt if you think it needs it.

4. Put the courgetti base in a bowl and pour over the sauce. Using your hands, toss everything together until the courgetti is completely coated in the sauce. It might be messy work, but it's worth it!

5. Divide between 4 bowls. Top with some lemon zest, a few mint leaves, chilli flakes if you can handle the spice, and finally a drizzle of olive oil.

This tells you how to present the dish.

When you see this symbol, turn to the next page to see more variations of the same recipe.

This is the list of tools you'll need.

Photos show you what the plant should look like at each stage.

☀ Grow in a sunny place · 🛠 Plant in spring

GROW YOUR OWN TOMATOES

Here's how to grow tasty tomatoes bursting with flavour – the type shown here are called "Hundreds and Thousands". Plant them somewhere that gets lots of light.

TOOLS
- Containers
- Seed compost
- Tomato seeds
- Large container with holes
- General purpose compost

1. Use seed compost to fill a container. Add the tomato seeds, then cover with more seed compost. Keep in a warm place, water well, and when you see leaves sprout, move to somewhere sunny.

2. Wait until 2 or 3 tomato plants have sprouted. Then take your large container with holes, and fill it with general purpose compost. Pop in your tomato plants, and cover the roots with more compost.

3. Place in a sunny position and keep your tomato plants well watered to help them grow. Wash before eating.

TIP
Use your tomatoes in these recipes.

29

GROW YOUR OWN

Learn how to grow your own fruit and vegetables on these pages. See p. 10 for all the tools you'll need.

Here are some of the recipes you can make using the ingredient you have grown.

KITCHEN RULES

Even though cooking can get a little messy, it's important to always think about cleanliness and safety while following each recipe. Read through all of these rules before getting started.

BE CAREFUL

This symbol means you're about to use something sharp or electrical. Take extra care, or ask an adult for help.

!

TOOLS AND INGREDIENTS

Before you start on a recipe, make sure you have all the tools you need. You might need to borrow them, or buy something new.

✷ Get all the ingredients ready. You may have some at home, but you may need to buy some.

✷ For recipes in this book, it's best to use large-sized eggs.

✷ Use whole, semi-skimmed, skimmed, or plant-based milk for recipes that require milk.

WEIGHTS AND MEASUREMENTS

Measure any ingredients you need before you start. Use tablespoons, teaspoons, scales, and a measuring jug as needed. Here's a guide to the abbreviations used in this cookbook:

METRIC

g = gram
kg = kilogram
ml = millilitre
l = litre

IMPERIAL

oz = ounce
lb = pound
fl oz = fluid ounce

GETTING STARTED

✷ Read the recipe all the way through before you begin.

✷ Roll up your sleeves, tie back long hair, and put on your favourite apron.

✷ Chop or slice anything that needs it.

SPOON MEASURES

tsp = teaspoon
tbsp = tablespoon

KITCHEN SAFETY

Make sure you enjoy yourself in the kitchen – but safety comes first. Follow these steps so that you don't hurt yourself. If you're not sure about anything, ask an adult to help.

⚔ Take extra care when peeling, grating, cutting, spiralizing, or using anything electrical.

⚔ Be very careful when cutting a large fruit or vegetable that has a thick skin, such as a watermelon. Cut it into quarters first, then cut off the peel before chopping into chunks.

⚔ Ask an adult for help if you don't feel confident or comfortable using a sharp knife.

⚔ Wipe up any spillages and tidy as you go.

⚔ Don't put your hands near the moving parts of an electrical tool, such as a food processor, unless you're absolutely certain it's switched off at the plug socket.

⚔ Wash your hands after handling anything spicy, such as chilli flakes, and avoid touching your mouth, eyes, or other sensitive areas.

SERVING SIZE

This tells you the final amount or the number of portions a recipe makes, or how many people it serves.

20 mins   Makes 4–6

PREPARATION TIME

This is how long a recipe will take to complete. It also tells you if you need to allow for extra time for extra preparation such as freezing or chilling.

KITCHEN HYGIENE

Follow these rules to prevent germs from spreading and to stop you from getting poorly.

⚔ Wash your hands before you start preparing food.

⚔ Wash all fruit and vegetables before using.

⚔ Use hot, soapy water to clean chopping boards between each use.

⚔ Check the use-by date on all ingredients.

⚔ Make sure the area where you are preparing food is kept clean.

⚔ Wash your hands after using raw eggs.

⚔ Please note that the Sweet mustard and dill sauce and the Semifreddos contain egg that isn't fully cooked. Don't serve these dishes to an elderly person, a baby, or a pregnant woman.

Cling film

Silver foil

Baking paper

Kitchen scissors

Serrated knife

Bread knife

Sharp knife

Table knife

Fork

Metal spoon

Salad servers

Wooden spoon

Whisk

Spatula

TOOLS

Here are all of the tools used in this cookbook.
Make sure you have the ones you need
ready before starting a recipe.

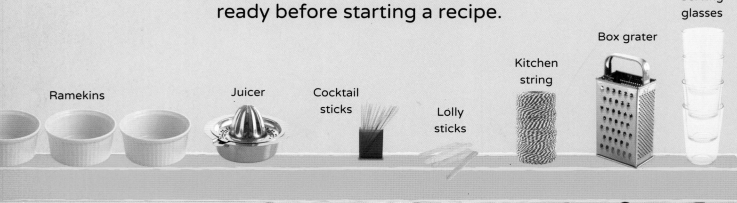

Ramekins

Juicer

Cocktail sticks

Lolly sticks

Kitchen string

Box grater

Serving glasses

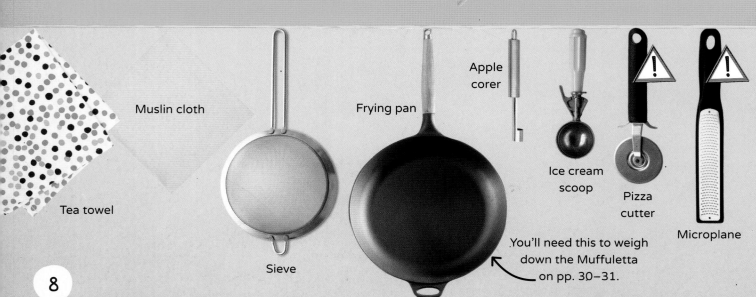

Muslin cloth

Tea towel

Sieve

Frying pan

Apple corer

Ice cream scoop

Pizza cutter

Microplane

You'll need this to weigh down the Muffuletta on pp. 30–31.

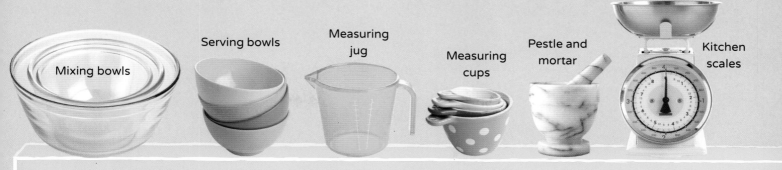

Mixing bowls

Serving bowls

Measuring jug

Measuring cups

Pestle and mortar

Kitchen scales

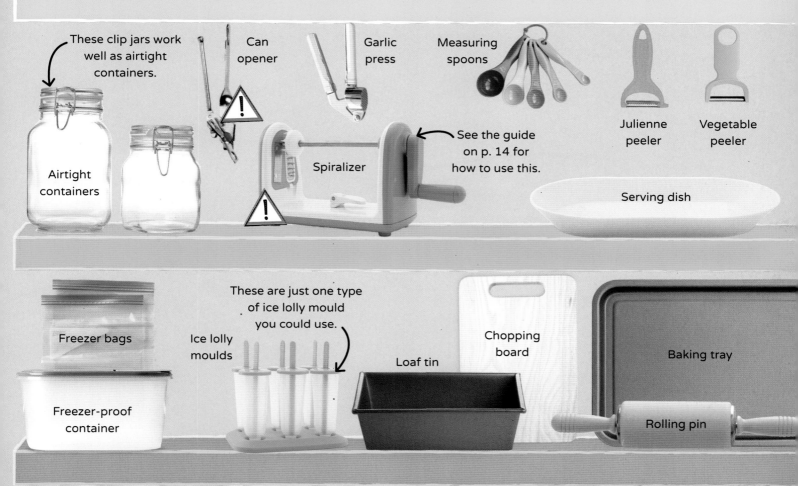

These clip jars work well as airtight containers.

Can opener

Garlic press

Measuring spoons

Julienne peeler

Vegetable peeler

Airtight containers

Spiralizer

See the guide on p. 14 for how to use this.

Serving dish

Freezer bags

These are just one type of ice lolly mould you could use.

Ice lolly moulds

Chopping board

Baking tray

Loaf tin

Freezer-proof container

Rolling pin

Food processor

Small food processor

Blender

Electric whisk

Kitchen paper

GARDENING EQUIPMENT

To grow the fruits and vegetables in this book, you'll need these handy pieces of equipment.

GETTING STARTED

Make sure you have the correct equipment before planting your seeds. Read the method through completely, so you know what you'll need for every stage.

Ruler

Pencil

Stapler

Scissors

Hessian bag

Plant pots

Strawberry plug

Liquid fertilizer

Bin liner

Straw

Gravel

Soil

Compost

WHEN TO PLANT

Look out for this symbol on each of the grow your own pages – it'll tell you the best time of year to start planting.

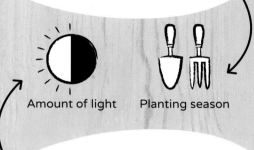

Amount of light   Planting season

WHERE TO GROW

This symbol tells you how much light each plant needs. All of the plants in this book can be grown in a garden, on a window sill, or on a balcony.

Seeds

Large container with drainage holes

Seed compost

General purpose compost

WHAT PLANTS NEED TO GROW

All plants need to be cared for to thrive. Different plants grow best in different conditions, but here are some general tips.

Time
All plants need time to grow. It might take a while for them to sprout leaves – so you have to be patient with them!

Temperature
Some plants, such as sunflowers, grow best in warm temperatures, while others like to be kept cool. Make sure you keep your plants at the temperature they need.

Water, air, and light
Plants need energy from food to grow. This energy is made in a process called photosynthesis. Plants use carbon dioxide gas from the air, water, and light from the sun to create their food.

Soil
Soil acts as an anchor for plants – it keeps their roots steady and secure while they grow. It also behaves like a sponge, absorbing water for the plant to soak up.

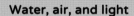

TECHNIQUES

Every good cook needs to master these basic techniques. They'll help you to prepare dishes easily and safely.

PEELERS

VEGETABLE PEELER

This is used to not only peel vegetables, such as carrots, but also to make crunchy vegetable ribbons. Remember to keep your fingers tucked away when peeling!

JULIENNE PEELER

This is like a vegetable peeler but it has little teeth instead of a flat blade. When used, the teeth drag down through vegetables to create very thin strips.

Carrot ribbons

1 To make vegetable ribbons and julienne strips, hold the vegetable firmly at an angle. If using carrots, peel the skin off first.

Julienned courgette

2 Drag the peeler downwards, giving the vegetable a quarter turn every three peels, so it peels evenly. Stop when you get to the seeds or the central core.

SHARP KNIFE

A sharp knife is often safer to use than a blunt one and it's an essential tool for any kitchen. Keep your knives sharp by hand washing and drying them as soon as you've finished using them. Never leave sharp knives in a sink full of water as someone could put their hand in and cut themselves.

HOW TO HOLD A KNIFE

Put a piece of damp kitchen paper under the chopping board. This will stop the board from slipping.

Grip the knife's handle firmly with the hand you write with. Your thumb and forefinger should rest on the top of the handle where it meets the blade.

BRIDGE TECHNIQUE

Hold big vegetables between your thumb and forefinger, making a bridge. Carefully cut down under the bridge.

CLAW TECHNIQUE

Tuck your fingertips in like a claw when slicing food. Even if your knife slips, it won't harm your hand.

Chop Try to chop the food into about 1–2 cm (0.4–0.8 in) wide pieces.

Finely chop Try to get the pieces as small as possible, roughly 0.5 cm (0.2 in) wide.

Dice If the recipe says to cube or dice, cut the food evenly in 1 cm (0.4 in) cubes.

Snip Herbs can be sliced any way you like. It's even easier to use scissors!

13

REMOVING AVOCADO STONES

1

Rest the avocado on a chopping board and use the claw technique to hold it with one hand. Use a small knife to cut all the way around the avocado until you feel the knife hit the stone.

2

Hold the top and bottom of the avocado with each hand. Gently twist the avocado halves to separate them.

3

Pull the two halves away from each other. Put the half without the stone to one side.

4

Use a spoon to scoop out the stone from the remaining half, and throw it away.

SPIRALIZER

If you don't have a spiralizer, you can use a julienne peeler to get a similar effect.

Spiralizers come in many shapes and sizes, but they all do the same job: turning firm vegetables, such as courgettes, into long, noodle-shaped spirals. Follow the instructions on the spiralizer you have.

BOX GRATER

A box grater has four different sides. Put it on a chopping board and hold the handle while you're working – this will keep the grater secure. Always grate down and away from your body, and watch your fingers!

TIP
Keep your grater sharp by only washing it by hand. Blunt graters can cause accidents.

LARGE GRATER

This is best for cheese, cucumber, and anything else you want in large pieces. If a recipe asks for something to be grated, this is the side to use.

SMALL GRATER

This side is great for Parmesan, ginger, and garlic. It produces small pieces of the food. If a recipe step needs you to finely grate something, use this side.

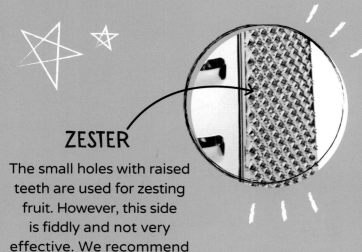

ZESTER

The small holes with raised teeth are used for zesting fruit. However, this side is fiddly and not very effective. We recommend using a microplane instead (see p. 17).

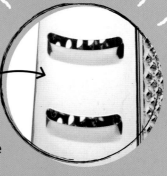

SLICER

You won't need this side while using this book, but it can slice apples or potatoes. It's quite tricky to master, so if you want to try using it, ask an adult to help.

SEPARATING EGG YOLKS AND WHITES

1

Crack the egg gently on a flat surface, or side of a bowl. Then, hold it upright and carefully prise the shell into halves – keep the contents of the egg in one half of the shell.

2

Hold the egg over a bowl and gently tip the yolk between the halves, so that the egg white drips into the bowl. Once the white is gone, pop the yolk into another bowl.

WHISKING

HAND WHISK

When using a hand whisk, it helps to slightly tilt the bowl you're using, and to whisk quickly and confidently.

ELECTRIC WHISK

Hold the bowl and slowly move the whisk while keeping it firmly in the mixture. It works quickly, so be careful not to overwhip.

JUICING CITRUS FRUIT

Using a juicer
Cut the fruit in half, then push onto the tip of the juicer flesh first. Twist the fruit around the tip, and keep pushing down to release its tasty juice.

Juicing by hand
Slice the fruit in half. Use one hand to squeeze it over a bowl. Cup your other hand under the fruit – the juice will run through your fingers, but you'll catch the pips.

FOLDING

Folding is a way of mixing two things together without knocking the air out. Use a large metal spoon in a gentle figure-of-eight motion, and slowly rotate the bowl so everything is mixed evenly. Always fold the thinner substance into the thicker one, not the other way round.

ZESTING WITH A MICROPLANE

You can use a microplane to finely grate ginger, too.

Rest the microplane on a chopping board and hold it at an angle. To zest, carefully rub the fruit over the microplane. Every so often, scrape the back of the microplane with a teaspoon to clear any zest that is stuck.

When zesting citrus fruit, stop when you get to the white pith under the skin. This tastes bitter and will spoil the food.

CRUSHING GARLIC

1

2

Put the garlic clove on a chopping board and carefully press down on it with the flat side of a knife. Once the skin has broken, it should peel off easily.

Trim the ends off the garlic clove, then put it in a garlic press. Squeeze the garlic press with both hands over a bowl. Use a teaspoon to scrape off any garlic that is stuck.

USING HERBS

Fresh herbs make food taste really flavourful.

TIP
Don't skimp on fresh herbs! They don't just taste good, they look beautiful too – especially fresh, soft herbs such as basil, mint, and coriander.

BASIL

If you're picking herbs from a plant, gently take from the top leaves and stems. Be careful not to bruise or damage the rest of the plant. This will encourage new leaves to grow.

COOKING INDEPENDENTLY

FOLLOWING RECIPES

Before you start cooking, read the recipe through completely so you know what you'll be doing. This should stop you from missing any tools, ingredients, or steps you need. If you have time, try to wash up a little as you go along – it will save you a job at the end and keep your kitchen nice and tidy.

COOKING WITHOUT HEAT

As these recipes don't use heat, it's easy to manage without an adult. Of course, if you're not sure about anything or need help with knife tasks, ask an adult. But, if you're careful and confident to do it alone, most of the recipes can be made from start to finish by yourself.

TRYING NEW THINGS

We've used many ingredients in this book – some you'll be familiar with and others that you might not be. It's important to be brave – you might end up not liking something, but that means you'll know for next time! Having an open mind about trying new things is a great life skill to learn.

NO-BAKE GRANOLA

This breakfast food is usually baked, but this no-cook version still gives you all of the fantastic flavours.

10 mins

Makes about 300g (10oz)

INGREDIENTS

- 150g (5½oz) unsweetened muesli with large toasted flakes
- 40g (1½oz) dried, toasted coconut flakes
- 30g (1oz) toasted flaked almonds
- 50g (1¾oz) sultanas
- 30g (1oz) roasted chopped hazelnuts

TOOLS

- Mixing bowl
- Scales
- Spoons
- Airtight container

TO SERVE

- Maple syrup
- Handful of fresh fruit
- 2–3 tbsp natural yogurt

1 To make the granola, just mix all the dry ingredients together. Keep it in an airtight container, somewhere cool and dry.

2 When ready to eat, weigh out a 40g (1½oz) portion of granola. Stir in 1 tsp of maple syrup, then top with your choice of fresh fruit and natural yogurt.

OVERNIGHT OATS

10 mins,
plus chilling

Each recipe
serves 4

These creamy oats are a filling breakfast. Make one of these toppings or choose your own!

INGREDIENTS

- 150g (5½oz) rolled jumbo oats
- 150ml (5fl oz) apple juice
- 150g (5½oz) natural yogurt
- 100–125ml (3½–4fl oz) water

TOOLS

- Scales
- Sharp knife
- Measuring jug
- Chopping board
- Spoons
- Mixing bowl
- Airtight containers
- Serving bowls

 1 Mix all of the ingredients together in an airtight container – only use 100ml (3½fl oz) water at this stage. Chill in the fridge overnight.

 2 The next day, give the oats a stir. If they feel very thick, add the remaining 25ml (1fl oz) water, or a splash of apple juice.

 3 When the overnight oats are ready to eat, prepare one of these tasty toppings.

JEWELLED OATS

INGREDIENTS

- 2 mangoes
- 300g (10oz) pomegranate seeds
- Handful of desiccated coconut
- Drizzle of honey, to serve

 1 ⚠ Carefully cut down the sides of a mango, avoiding the stone. Lay the mango skin side down, and use a spoon to scoop the flesh out of the skin. Repeat for the second mango.

 2 ⚠ Finely chop the mango flesh into chunks. Put most of the mango pieces and pomegranate seeds into the overnight oats and stir through.

 3 Divide the oats into 4 bowls. Scatter the remaining fruit and some desiccated coconut on top. Drizzle over some honey and tuck in.

AUTUMN OATS

BERRY AND CHERRY OATS

INGREDIENTS

- 2 pears
- 150g (5½oz) blueberries
- Pinch of ground cinnamon, plus extra to top

1. Finely chop 1 pear. Mix the chopped pear with the overnight oats, then stir in some of the blueberries and the cinnamon.

2. Carefully cut the second pear into quarters. Slice each piece of pear lengthways 5 times, and arrange the slices in a fan shape.

3. Divide the oats into 4 bowls, then top with a pear fan, the rest of the blueberries, and an extra dusting of cinnamon.

INGREDIENTS

- 8 strawberries
- 24 raspberries
- Dash of vanilla extract
- 12 cherries, stones removed
- Handful of flaked almonds

1. Finely chop the strawberries. Put all of the chopped strawberries, the raspberries, and the vanilla extract into the overnight oats and stir through.

2. Divide the oats between 4 bowls, then top with cherries and the flaked almonds.

CHANGE IT UP!
To make an **apple crumble flavour**, try adding some finely chopped apple, a drizzle of maple syrup, a pinch of nutmeg, sultanas, and hazelnuts to the oats.

BREAKFAST SMOOTHIES

Almost everyone loves smoothies! They are full of fresh fruit and vegetables. Here are 5 flavours to try…

INGREDIENTS

- 100g (3½oz) spinach
- 1 banana, peeled and roughly chopped
- 4 dates, stones removed
- 40g (1½oz) roasted chopped hazelnuts
- 200ml (7fl oz) apple juice
- 2 pears, roughly chopped

GREEN GOODNESS

INGREDIENTS

- 300g (10oz) frozen forest fruits
- 100g (3½oz) unsweetened muesli
- 200ml (7fl oz) milk
- ½–1 tbsp maple syrup
- Juice of ½ a lemon

FOREST FRUITS

PB&J

TOOLS

- Spoons
- Scales
- Measuring jug
- Blender
- Chopping board
- Sharp knife
- Paper straws
- Mixing bowl

1 Put the mixing bowl on the scales and reset the scales to zero. Weigh the ingredients in the bowl, resetting the scales to zero each time you add a new ingredient.

2 ⚠ Measure anything you can't weigh separately, such as milk or juice, then pour all of the ingredients into the blender. Blend everything together until there are no lumps.

3 If your blender has trouble whizzing any fruit, add a little more milk, water, or juice. Pour into glasses and serve with a paper straw.

INGREDIENTS

- 300g (10oz) raspberries
- 60g (2oz) peanut butter
- 200ml (7fl oz) orange juice
- 1 tbsp clear honey
- 1 banana, peeled and roughly chopped

INGREDIENTS

- 150g (5½oz) strawberries
- 150g (5½oz) mango chunks
- 200ml (7fl oz) orange juice
- 1 banana, peeled and roughly chopped
- 1 tsp clear honey

INGREDIENTS

- 50g (1¾oz) sachet of creamed coconut
- 300g (10oz) pineapple chunks
- 200ml (7fl oz) milk
- 1 banana, peeled and roughly chopped

TIP

These smoothies will keep covered in the fridge for up to 2 days. Give them a stir before serving.

SUNSET SMOOTHIE

TOTALLY TROPICAL

Once you're an expert at making smoothies, try out these different ways to serve them.

20 mins, plus freezing

Makes 4

SMOOTHIE BOWLS

TOOLS

- Spoons
- Scales
- Chopping board
- Sharp knife
- Food processor

1 Choose any smoothie flavour from pp. 24–25.

2 Before you start, freeze any fruit that's needed for up to 12 hours.

3 Once the fruit is frozen, pop it into the food processor with the other ingredients. Use about 50ml (2fl oz) less fruit juice or milk than in the smoothie recipe, as the mixture needs to be nice and thick.

4 ⚠ Whizz everything together in the food processor.

5 Pour the mixture into 4 bowls, then decorate with your choice of toppings – try fresh fruit, nuts, seeds, coconut flakes, chocolate chips, or even edible flowers!

SMOOTHIE POPS

15 mins,
plus freezing

Makes 18

TOOLS

- Jugs
- 90ml (3fl oz) capacity ice lolly moulds
- Lolly sticks
- Freezer-proof containers

1 Choose any 3 smoothie flavours from pp. 24–25, and make them using the method on the same page.

2 Pop each smoothie in the freezer for roughly 20 minutes, then transfer each smoothie to a jug. Pour them slowly, one after the other, into ice lolly moulds. Be careful not to pour too quickly, or the colours will run into each other.

3 Put the lolly sticks into the smoothie-filled moulds, then freeze for at least 6 hours, or for up to 1 week.

4 When the smoothie pops are frozen and ready to eat, run each lolly mould under warm water until you can pull the lolly free.

TIP
You can also make smoothie pops with just 1 smoothie flavour. You'll end up with 6 pops instead of 18, and you won't need to freeze the smoothie before pouring it into the moulds.

Grow in a sunny place

Plant in spring

GROW YOUR OWN
TOMATOES

Here's how to grow tasty tomatoes bursting with flavour – the type shown here are called "Hundreds and Thousands". Plant them somewhere that gets lots of light.

TOOLS

- Containers
- Seed compost
- Tomato seeds
- Large container with holes
- General purpose compost

1

Use seed compost to fill a container. Add the tomato seeds, then cover with more seed compost. Keep in a warm place, water well, and when you see leaves sprout, move to somewhere sunny.

2

Wait until 2 or 3 tomato plants have sprouted. Then take your large container with holes, and fill it with general purpose compost. Pop in your tomato plants, and cover the roots with more compost.

3

Place in a sunny position and keep your tomato plants well watered to help them grow. Wash before eating.

TIP

Use your tomatoes in these recipes.

Indian sharing Platter
PP. 58—59

Chickpea and tomato
salad PP. 36—37

Smashed avocado
PP. 34—35

30 mins,
plus resting

Serves 6–8

MUFFULETTA

This enormous round sandwich from New Orleans, USA, looks like a regular loaf of bread. However, when it's cut into wedges, you'll see layers and layers of colourful filling inside.

TOOLS

- Serrated knife
- Chopping board
- Small food processor
- Scales
- Teaspoon
- Cling film
- Baking tray
- Sieve
- Frying pan

INGREDIENTS

- 1 round cob or bloomer loaf, about 18 cm (7 in) measured across the base
- 150g (5½oz) sunblush tomatoes, drained
- 145g (5oz) fresh basil pesto
- 200g (7oz) wafer-thin ham
- 150g (5½oz) smoked cheese slices
- 100g (3½oz) salami
- 20g (¾oz) basil leaves
- 280g (9½oz) jar roasted red peppers, drained and patted dry

1

Use the knife to cut off the top third of the loaf. Scoop out the insides with your hands, leaving a thin layer of bread inside.

2

Whizz the tomatoes to a paste in the food processor and set aside. Using the back of a teaspoon, spread the pesto inside the loaf and its lid, then repeat with the tomato paste.

3

At the bottom of the loaf, layer up half of the ham, half of the cheese, and half the salami. Next, top with the basil leaves and all of the peppers. Finally, top with the remaining salami, cheese, and ham. Pack each layer in tightly and evenly.

4

Put the lid back on the loaf, then wrap in cling film and put on a baking tray. Weigh down with a frying pan and transfer to the fridge for about 6 hours, or until the loaf has flattened slightly.

5 ⚠ To serve, remove the cling film, then carefully slice the loaf into wedges.

TIP
Keep the insides of the loaf to make Panzanella (see pp. 88–89).

20 mins

Serves 4

NECTARINE AND FETA SALAD

CHANGE IT UP!
You can substitute the nectarines for other fruits, such as cherries, peaches, or apples.

This colourful dish goes well with homemade honey mustard dressing. The almonds add some crunch – an essential part of any good salad!

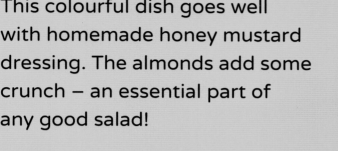

TOOLS

- Scales
- Jar with lid
- Sharp knife
- Chopping board
- Spoons
- Serving dish
- Salad servers
- Pestle and mortar

INGREDIENTS

- 3 nectarines
- 110g (4oz) salad leaves
- 100g (3½oz) feta cheese
- Large handful of almonds

FOR THE DRESSING

- 1 tbsp wholegrain mustard
- 1 tbsp sherry vinegar, or rice wine vinegar
- 2 tsp clear honey
- 3 tbsp olive oil

TIP
This recipe makes enough dressing for 2 salads. You can keep it sealed in the fridge for up to 1 week.

1 To make the dressing, put the mustard, vinegar, and honey in the jar with a pinch of salt. Make sure the lid is on tightly, then shake until everything is mixed together.

2 Pour in the olive oil, then put the lid back on. Shake the jar again, until everything is combined and the dressing has thickened. Set aside.

3 Use a sharp knife to carefully cut down each side of 1 nectarine until you're left with 4 large pieces and the stone. Cut each piece into thin slices, and throw away the stone. Repeat for the remaining nectarines.

4 Put the salad leaves into the serving dish and top with the nectarine slices. Use your hands to crumble over the feta cheese.

5 Roughly crush the almonds in the pestle and mortar. Scatter most of the crushed almonds into the serving dish.

6 Drizzle over about half of the dressing, and toss everything together with the salad servers. Sprinkle on the rest of the almonds, then enjoy!

10 mins

 Serves 1

SMASHED AVOCADO

This can be made in minutes – it's perfect for a quick lunch. The smooth avocado and sweet pumpernickel bread will keep you feeling full all afternoon.

TOOLS

- Chopping board
- Bread knife
- Sharp knife
- Table knife
- Mixing bowl
- Vegetable peeler
- Fork
- Juicer
- Spoon

INGREDIENTS

- 1 small, ripe avocado
- Juice of ½ a lime
- 1 slice pumpernickel bread
- 1 medium tomato, sliced
- Parmesan cheese
- 6–8 small mint leaves, to serve
- Extra virgin olive oil, to serve

TIP

To check whether an avocado is ripe, squeeze it gently – it should feel a little bit soft. If it's still hard, it needs a few more days to ripen.

See p. 14 for how to cut open an avocado and remove the stone. Use a spoon to scoop out the avocado flesh, then pop it in the mixing bowl.

 Cut the slice of pumpernickel bread in half. Spread the smashed avocado over each half, then top with tomato slices.

 Squeeze the lime juice into the bowl and add a generous pinch of salt. Mash with a fork until most of the lumps have gone.

 Use the vegetable peeler to peel some Parmesan shavings, then add those to the sandwich. Scatter over mint leaves and drizzle with a little olive oil. Gobble it up immediately!

CHANGE IT UP!

Try using different flavoured oils to drizzle over the top, such as garlic, chilli, or basil. You can also use any type of bread you like.

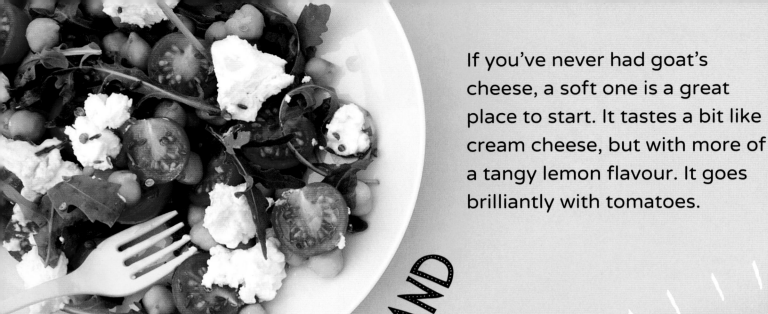

If you've never had goat's cheese, a soft one is a great place to start. It tastes a bit like cream cheese, but with more of a tangy lemon flavour. It goes brilliantly with tomatoes.

CHICKPEA AND TOMATO SALAD

15 mins, plus marinating

Serves 4

TOOLS

- Serrated knife
- Can opener
- Chopping board
- Spoons
- Scales
- Serving plate
- Salad servers
- Sieve
- Pestle and mortar

INGREDIENTS

- 300g (10oz) cherry tomatoes
- 2 tsp red wine vinegar
- ¼ tsp sugar
- 3 tbsp extra virgin olive oil
- 400g (14oz) can of chickpeas
- ½ tbsp cumin seeds
- ½ tbsp coriander seeds
- 50g (1¾oz) rocket leaves
- 75g (2½oz) soft, rindless goat's cheese

1 Carefully cut the cherry tomatoes in half. Put them on the serving plate with the red wine vinegar, sugar, olive oil, and a pinch of salt.

 2 Open the can of chickpeas and tip them into a sieve over a sink. Rinse well with cold water, then shake the sieve to get rid of any extra water. Tip onto the serving plate.

 3 Stir everything together and leave to marinate (soak together) for about 25 minutes. The tomato juices will begin to mix with the vinegar and oil.

 4 Gently crush the cumin and coriander seeds in the pestle and mortar. When you're ready to serve, add the rocket leaves and crushed spices to the serving plate.

5 Using your fingers, gently crumble the goat's cheese over the top. Toss everything together using salad servers, then enjoy!

Grow in a
sunny place

Plant in spring
to summer

GROW YOUR OWN
LETTUCE

1 Use the pencil to make a few holes roughly 1.5 cm (½ in) deep in a plant pot filled with seed compost. Sprinkle some lettuce seeds in each hole. Cover with more compost, then water.

2 Pull out some leaves once the lettuce plants start to sprout. Keep well watered.

3 To stop pesky slugs from eating the leaves, pour some gravel on the soil around the plant when it reaches roughly this size.

4

If the weather is warm, you'll need to water this plant once or twice a day. When you want to eat some lettuce, only pick the outer leaves off the plant. Wash and enjoy!

TIP
Use your lettuce in these recipes.

Chopped salad
PP. 46—47

Seafood handrolls
PP. 92—93

Coronation chicken
Picnic baguette P. 47

Lettuce comes in many different varieties, so plant your favourite. Watch the leaves — they will keep growing and growing!

PICNIC BAGUETTES

20 mins

Each recipe serves 6–8

These sandwiches are packed with fantastic flavours and are great to make for a picnic. Take your pick from these fillings, or make them all!

INGREDIENTS

- 1 baguette, or French stick
- 2 tbsp butter, softened

BRIE, PEAR, AND ROCKET

You can squeeze lemon juice on the pear to stop it turning brown quickly.

INGREDIENTS

- 1–2 tbsp sweet chilli sauce
- 7–10 slices of brie
- 10–12 slices of pear
- Large handful of rocket leaves
- Juice of ½ a lemon (optional)

1 Spread the sweet chilli sauce all along the baguette. Fill with slices of brie, pear, and rocket leaves.

INGREDIENTS

- 40g (1½oz) mayonnaise
- 20g (¾oz) ketchup
- 5–6 drops of Worcestershire sauce
- Juice of ½ a lemon
- 175g (6oz) cooked North Atlantic prawns
- Handful of watercress
- Handful of prawn crackers, to serve

TOOLS

- Bread knife
- Table knife
- Baking paper, or silver foil
- Scissors
- Spoons
- Kitchen paper
- Scales
- Mixing bowls

1 Carefully slice the baguette lengthways three-quarters of the way through. Don't cut the baguette fully in half.

2 Spread butter along the baguette, then stuff with your choice of filling. Don't make it too full though, or things will ooze out!

3 Wrap it up in foil or baking paper, and keep it in the fridge until you're ready for your picnic.

PRAWN COCKTAIL

1 Put the mayonnaise, ketchup, Worcestershire sauce, and lemon juice in a bowl. Season with salt and pepper then mix together.

2 Pat the prawns dry with kitchen paper, then stir into the sauce. Put a layer of watercress along the baguette, then spoon in the prawn mixture. Add prawn crackers for an extra crunch!

CORONATION CHICKEN

INGREDIENTS

- Handful of little gem lettuce leaves
- Handful of cucumber, sliced
- 250g (9oz) pre-cooked chicken breasts, shredded
- 40g (1½oz) Greek yogurt
- 40g (1½oz) mayonnaise
- 1 tsp medium curry powder
- ¼ tsp turmeric
- 1 tbsp mango chutney
- 10g (¼oz) mint leaves, finely chopped

1 Line the baguette with the lettuce leaves and cucumber slices. Mix together the other ingredients, then fill the baguette and enjoy.

MINTY PEA SOUP

This refreshing, bright green soup is perfect for hot days, as it is served cold!

10 mins Serves 4

TOOLS

- Scales
- Measuring jug
- Blender
- Spoons
- Bowls

INGREDIENTS

- 400g (14oz) frozen peas, defrosted, plus extra to garnish
- 500ml (16fl oz) chicken stock
- 100g (3½oz) crusty white bread, torn into small chunks, plus extra to serve
- 24 mint leaves
- Juice of 1 lemon
- 1 tbsp crème fraîche
- 4 pre-cooked bacon rashers, roughly chopped (omit for vegetarians)
- Extra virgin olive oil, to drizzle

TIP

Try to use a liquid stock so you don't have to boil the kettle, but if you only have a stock cube, you can use that instead. Ask an adult to pour boiling water over the stock cube in a jug until you have 500ml (16fl oz) of stock. Stir until there are no lumps.

CHANGE IT UP!

If you're vegetarian, use vegetable stock instead of chicken stock, and add some lemon zest to replace the bacon.

1 ⚠ Before starting, make sure that the frozen peas are fully defrosted. Put the peas, chicken stock, bread, 12 mint leaves, and lemon juice into the blender and whizz until smooth.

2 ⚠ If the mixture is quite thick, add up to 200ml (7fl oz) cold water and blend again until it reaches a soup-like texture.

3 Stir through the crème fraîche and season with salt and pepper, then divide between 4 bowls.

4 Garnish with a few peas, the rest of the mint leaves, bits of crispy bacon, and a drizzle of olive oil. Serve with chunks of bread for dipping!

CAULIFLOWER RICE BOWL

30 mins

Serves 4

Rice bowls are usually made with sticky sushi rice. This version uses whizzed up cauliflower instead, which means you don't have to do any cooking!

TOOLS

- Scales
- Mixing bowls
- Food processor
- Chopping board
- Sharp knife
- Table knife
- Vegetable peeler
- Spoons

INGREDIENTS

- 1 medium cauliflower
- 4 tbsp rice vinegar
- 2 tsp caster sugar
- 2 avocados
- Juice of ½ a lime
- 120g (4oz) frozen edamame beans, defrosted
- 2 carrots, peeled and grated
- 8 radishes, thinly sliced
- 2 spring onions, halved and thinly sliced
- 100g (3½oz) smoked salmon slices
- 2 nori (seaweed) sheets, torn into large pieces

TO SERVE

- 2 tsp sesame seeds
- Coriander leaves
- Lime wedges
- Soy sauce

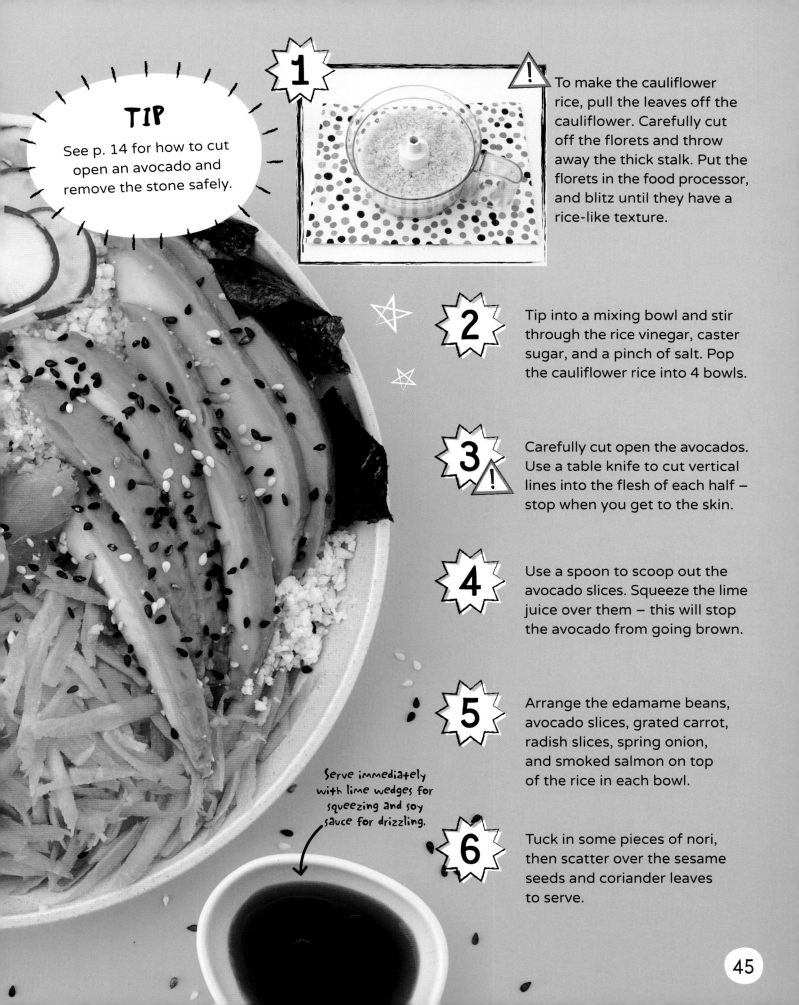

TIP

See p. 14 for how to cut open an avocado and remove the stone safely.

1 ⚠ To make the cauliflower rice, pull the leaves off the cauliflower. Carefully cut off the florets and throw away the thick stalk. Put the florets in the food processor, and blitz until they have a rice-like texture.

2 Tip into a mixing bowl and stir through the rice vinegar, caster sugar, and a pinch of salt. Pop the cauliflower rice into 4 bowls.

3 ⚠ Carefully cut open the avocados. Use a table knife to cut vertical lines into the flesh of each half – stop when you get to the skin.

4 Use a spoon to scoop out the avocado slices. Squeeze the lime juice over them – this will stop the avocado from going brown.

5 Arrange the edamame beans, avocado slices, grated carrot, radish slices, spring onion, and smoked salmon on top of the rice in each bowl.

Serve immediately with lime wedges for squeezing and soy sauce for drizzling.

6 Tuck in some pieces of nori, then scatter over the sesame seeds and coriander leaves to serve.

TOOLS

- Chopping board
- Sharp knife
- Can opener
- Sieve
- Pestle and mortar
- Scales
- Garlic press
- Mixing bowl
- Spoons
- Serving bowl
- Salad servers

INGREDIENTS

- 2 celery sticks, ends trimmed
- 100g (3½oz) Cheddar cheese, or other
- ½ cucumber
- 100g (3½oz) radishes, tops trimmed
- 1 romaine lettuce, end trimmed
- 400g (14oz) can of chickpeas
- 100g (3½oz) macadamia nuts

FOR THE DRESSING

- 150g (5½oz) soured cream
- 30g (1oz) mayonnaise
- ¼ tsp paprika
- 1 small garlic clove, crushed
- Juice of ½ a lemon
- 10g (¼oz) chives, finely chopped

CHOPPED SALAD

15 mins,
plus resting

Serves 4

This creamy, vegetable-packed salad is an excellent way to practise your chopping skills.

 1 Carefully cut the celery sticks in half lengthways, then cut each half into small pieces, roughly 1 cm (0.4 in) thick.

 **2** Cut the cheese into cubes similar in size to the celery pieces.

 3 Carefully slice the cucumber in half lengthways, then use a teaspoon to scrape the seeds out of each half. Cut each half into 4 strips, then chop the strips into small pieces, roughly 1 cm (0.4 in) thick.

4 Carefully cut the radishes into pieces similar in size to the cucumber, then carefully slice the romaine lettuce into thin strips, roughly 1 cm (0.4 in) wide.

 5 Open the can of chickpeas and drain using the sieve. Rinse well with cold water, then shake to get rid of any excess water. Tip the chickpeas into the serving bowl, along with all of the chopped vegetables.

 6 Put the nuts in the pestle and mortar and crush until the biggest pieces are roughly the same size as the chickpeas, then transfer to the serving bowl.

 7 Mix the dressing ingredients in a bowl with some salt and pepper. Pour into the serving bowl and toss with the salad servers – everything should be covered in dressing. Leave to stand for 20 minutes to let the flavours mix together, then serve.

CHANGE IT UP!

To make this vegetarian, don't use the anchovies in the dressing, swap the chicken and bacon for sliced avocado, and use vegetarian Parmesan.

INGREDIENTS

- 2 pre-cooked chicken breasts, shredded
- 2 cos lettuce hearts, roughly chopped
- 60g (2oz) Parmesan shavings
- 10g (¼oz) chives, roughly chopped
- 100g (3½oz) croutons
- 4 pre-cooked bacon rashers, roughly chopped

FOR THE DRESSING

- 80g (3oz) mayonnaise
- 1 tsp Dijon mustard
- 4 salted anchovy fillets, drained and patted dry
- ½ garlic clove, crushed
- Juice of 1 lemon

The anchovies in the dressing don't have a very strong flavour, but you can leave them out if you don't like them.

CHICKEN CAESAR SALAD

Whip up this salad as a light lunch or as a side dish for dinner. Yum!

25 mins

Serves 4

TOOLS

- Sharp knife
- Chopping board
- Scales
- Garlic press
- Sieve
- Mini food processor
- Spoons
- Serving bowl
- Salad servers

1 To make the dressing, put all of the ingredients, except for the lemon juice, into the mini food processor. Whizz until smooth.

2 Squeeze the lemon juice into the food processor. Add some cold water, so that the dressing can be thickly poured (the exact amount of water will depend on what mayonnaise you use).

3 Put all of the salad ingredients in a bowl. Drizzle over the dressing and toss everything together, so that the leaves are evenly coated. Serve right away, before the leaves go soggy!

15 mins   **Serves 6**

GAZPACHO

This colourful, cold vegetable soup comes from Spain. Grab some crusty bread to dip in it and cool down on a hot day!

TOOLS

- Mixing bowl
- Blender
- Spoons
- Scales
- Vegetable peeler
- Measuring jug
- Chopping board
- Sharp knife
- Serving bowls

INGREDIENTS

- 160g (6oz) stale crusty bread
- 1 cucumber, peeled and diced into cubes
- 1kg (2¼lb) ripe tomatoes, roughly chopped
- 1 red pepper, roughly chopped and deseeded
- 1 green pepper, roughly chopped and deseeded
- 2 small garlic cloves
- 2 tbsp sherry vinegar
- 150ml (5fl oz) extra virgin olive oil, plus extra to drizzle
- 8 pitted black olives, to serve
- Handful of basil leaves, to serve

TIP
This is a great soup for a picnic. Chill it for a few hours in the fridge, then transfer to a flask to take with you.

 1 Tear the bread into rough pieces. Fill the mixing bowl with cold water and briefly dunk each chunk of bread into it, just long enough so that it absorbs some water.

 2 Lift the bread out and gently squeeze it to remove any excess water, then put into the blender.

3 Add most of the cucumber and chopped tomatoes, all of the peppers, the garlic cloves, sherry vinegar, and olive oil to the blender.

 4 Season with some salt and black pepper, then blitz until the soup is completely smooth. Divide the gazpacho into 6 bowls.

 5 Carefully slice the olives. Top the soup with the remaining cucumber and tomatoes, the olives, and the basil leaves. Finish with a drizzle of olive oil.

 6 Eat right away, or don't add the toppings and pop the soup in an airtight container in the fridge for up to 2 days.

Serves 4

COUSCOUS AND SPINACH SALAD

This recipe is delicious on its own, but is also excellent to serve with cooked meat or fish.

TOOLS

- Mixing bowl
- Measuring jug
- Plate
- Scales
- Spoons
- Fork
- Chopping board
- Sharp knife

INGREDIENTS

- 100g (3½oz) couscous
- 180ml (6fl oz) water
- 1 red pepper
- 150g (5½oz) cherry tomatoes
- 2 large handfuls of spinach, finely chopped

TO SERVE

- 1 tbsp extra virgin olive oil
- Lemon wedges

1 Put the couscous in a mixing bowl with 180ml (6fl oz) cold water. Cover with a plate and leave for about 30–40 minutes, or until the couscous has puffed up and all the water has disappeared.

2 Add a pinch of salt to the couscous, then use the fork to stir it through and fluff it up. Set aside.

3 ⚠ Carefully slice 4 sides off the red pepper and discard the leftover seeds and stalk. Cut away any white bits from inside the pepper pieces, then slice into thin strips. Cut each strip into small cubes.

4 ⚠ Carefully cut the cherry tomatoes into quarters. Add them and the red pepper cubes into the couscous bowl along with the spinach. Stir well to mix.

TO SERVE

Drizzle over the olive oil, add some salt and pepper, then mix everything together. Either cover and keep in the fridge for up to 12 hours, or serve immediately with the lemon wedges.

Grow in a
sunny place

Plant
in spring
to summer

GROW YOUR OWN
CARROTS

 1 Carefully staple the bin liner inside the hessian bag. Then, poke a few holes at the bottom of the bin liner – this will help to drain away any excess water.

 2 Fill the bag with compost and make shallow trenches in the top of the compost. Scatter the carrot seeds in the trenches, then cover with more compost.

 3 As the carrot plants grow, thin them out by pulling out about half of the plants – there should be a gap of roughly 5 cm (2 in) between each plant. This gives the plants space to grow.

 4 Water the carrot plants often and give them a liquid fertilizer once a week when the leaves begin to grow. They should be big and ready to wash and eat after about 12 weeks.

When you think about carrots, you probably picture orange ones. However, these pointy vegetables come in many different shapes and colours!

TOOLS

- Hessian bag
- Bin liner
- Stapler
- Carrot seeds
- Compost
- Liquid fertilizer

TIP

Use your carrots in these recipes.

Cauliflower rice bowl pp. 44—45

Prawn summer rolls pp. 82—83

Sesame coleslaw p. 85

DIP POTS

These different coloured dips are perfect for dunking nibbles, such as breadsticks and raw vegetables.

TOMATO HUMMUS

Makes 450g (1lb)

INGREDIENTS

- 120g (4oz) sunblush tomatoes, drained
- 400g (14oz) can of chickpeas, drained and rinsed
- ½ garlic clove, crushed
- 3 tbsp olive oil

1 Put all the ingredients in a food processor and whizz everything until smooth. Season with salt and pepper. Divide into ramekins, and serve immediately.

CREAMY CHIVE DIP

Makes 200g (7oz)

INGREDIENTS

- 100g (3½oz) mayonnaise
- 100g (3½oz) Greek yogurt
- 10g (¼oz) chives, finely snipped

1 Mix all the ingredients together and season with salt and pepper. Spoon into ramekins, and serve with thinly sliced vegetables and breadsticks.

TOOLS

- Food processor
- Spoons
- Scales
- Scissors
- Garlic press
- Sieve
- Small glasses
- Ramekins

30 mins

TO SERVE

- Basil leaves
- Thinly sliced vegetables, such as red peppers, cucumber, or carrots
- Breadsticks

PEA AND BASIL PURÉE

LAYERED DIPS

For a snazzy look, layer the dips in serving glasses.

1 Spoon a layer of each dip into a serving glass. Start with the pea and basil purée, then a thin layer of the chive dip, and finally the tomato hummus. Repeat for more serving glasses. Top with basil leaves and serve.

Makes 450g (1lb)

INGREDIENTS

- 400g (14oz) frozen peas, fully defrosted
- 3 tbsp olive oil
- Large handful of basil leaves

1 ⚠ Put all the ingredients in a food processor and whizz until you have a smooth purée. Season with salt and pepper. Pop into ramekins, and serve with vegetables and breadsticks.

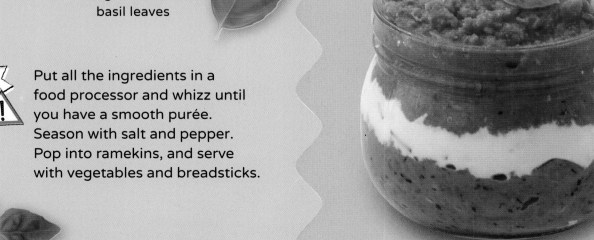

INDIAN SHARING PLATTER

30 mins, plus soaking

Serves 4

The dishes here are inspired by Indian food. They are full of different flavours and textures and are made to be shared. Grab a bit of everything and tuck in.

TOOLS

- Box grater
- Mixing bowls
- Pestle and mortar
- Scales
- Measuring jug
- Spoons
- Chopping board
- Sharp knife
- Serving bowls

TO SERVE

- Mango chutney
- Pomegranate seeds
- 2 handfuls of Bombay mix, roughly crushed in a pestle and mortar
- Poppadoms

FOR THE SALAD

- ½ red onion, finely chopped
- Juice of 1 lemon
- Pinch of caster sugar
- ½ cucumber, diced
- 3 medium tomatoes, diced
- 1 tsp cumin seeds

1 Put the red onion and lemon juice in a bowl with the sugar and a pinch of salt. Stir and then leave to soak for 20 minutes.

2 Add the remaining ingredients to the bowl, mix well, then season with more salt and set aside.

FOR THE COCONUT PANEER

- 40g (1½oz) desiccated coconut
- 60ml (2fl oz) water
- 8 green cardamom pods
- 110g (4oz) paneer cheese, grated
- 1 tbsp black onion seeds
- ½ tsp turmeric
- Juice of 1 lime
- 2 spring onions, thinly sliced
- Pinch of mild chilli powder
- ½ tbsp sunflower oil
- 10g (¼oz) coriander leaves, roughly chopped

1 Put the desiccated coconut in a small bowl with 60ml (2fl oz) water. Stir, then leave to soak for 20 minutes to fluff it up!

2 Once the coconut has soaked up all of the water, put the cardamom pods in the pestle and mortar. Bash them a couple of times to break the pods apart.

3 Using your fingers, pick out the black seeds from inside the pods and throw away the pods. Put the seeds back in the pestle and mortar and finely crush.

4 Mix together the crushed seeds and coconut with all the other ingredients. Season with a pinch of salt and set aside.

TO SERVE

Put everything in separate bowls on a large platter, or the table. Add some of each dish to your plate and scoop up with poppadoms!

FOR THE RAITA

- ½ cucumber
- 200g (7oz) full-fat natural yogurt
- 20 mint leaves, roughly chopped

1 ⚠ Carefully slice the cucumber in half lengthways, then drag a teaspoon along the seeds to scoop them out.

2 Grate the cucumber into a bowl. Spoon in the yogurt, then stir in the mint leaves. Mix together and set aside.

PANCAKE SPIRALS

25 mins **Makes 24**

These nectarine, ricotta, and honey bites are so easy to make. Make sure you roll them up tightly so the filling doesn't fall out!

TOOLS

- Sharp knife
- Chopping board
- Table knife
- Spoons

INGREDIENTS

- 2 nectarines
- 4 crêpes, pre-made
- 4 tbsp ricotta cheese
- 4 tsp clear honey

1

Use the sharp knife to carefully cut down each side of the nectarine, until you're left with large pieces and the stone. Cut each chunk into thin slices, and throw away the stone. Repeat for the other nectarine.

2

Leave some room at the top and bottom of the pancake to help you roll it.

Lay a crêpe on the chopping board and spread over 1 tbsp of ricotta cheese. Arrange some nectarine slices on top (about half a nectarine per crêpe) then drizzle over 1 tsp of clear honey.

3

Starting at the bottom, roll up the crêpe as tightly as you can, being careful not to rip it. Once it's rolled up, carefully slice the top and bottom off to straighten the ends, then cut into 6 equal pieces.

4

Repeat steps 2 and 3 with the remaining crêpes, then enjoy! You can cover and keep these fruit-filled spirals in the fridge for up to 1 day.

FRUIT AND CHEESE KEBABS

These yummy skewers are packed full of flavour – they are both sweet and savoury.

TOOLS

- Cocktail sticks
- Sharp knife
- Chopping board
- Scales
- Pestle and mortar
- Spoons

15 mins

Each recipe makes 6

WATERMELON, FETA, AND PEANUT

INGREDIENTS

- 60g (2oz) feta cheese, cut into 6 cubes
- 6 mint leaves
- 120g (4oz) watermelon, cut into 6 triangles
- 1 tbsp salted peanuts, to serve

 1 Thread each cube of feta cheese onto a cocktail stick. Pop 1 mint leaf on each stick. Finish each kebab with a watermelon triangle.

 2 Put the peanuts in the pestle and mortar and roughly crush them. Arrange the kebabs on a plate, then sprinkle over the crushed peanuts and serve immediately.

APPLE, CHEDDAR, AND GRAPE

INGREDIENTS

- 60g (2oz) Cheddar cheese
- ½ apple
- 6 red grapes
- 1 sprig of thyme, leaves picked, to serve

 Carefully cut the Cheddar cheese into 6 cubes and slice the apple half into 6 wedges.

 Thread a grape, followed by a cube of cheese, and then an apple wedge onto each cocktail stick. Arrange on a plate, scatter over the thyme leaves, and serve immediately.

NECTARINE, PARMA HAM, AND MOZZARELLA

INGREDIENTS

- 6 mini mozzarella cheese balls
- 6 basil leaves
- 2 slices Parma ham
- 1 nectarine

 Push a mozzarella ball onto each cocktail stick, then add a basil leaf.

 Tear each slice of Parma ham into 3 pieces. Fold each piece 2–3 times so they're roughly the same size as the mozzarella balls, then thread those on.

 Use a sharp knife to cut the nectarine in half, remove the stone with a teaspoon, then cut each half into 3 wedges.

 Thread the nectarine wedges onto the cocktail sticks. Serve immediately.

NUTTY RED PEPPER PURÉE

This bright orange dish is a simple snack with a nutty flavour. It comes from Spain and is great to dip fresh vegetables in, or you can spread it on crackers.

20 mins

Serves 6–8

TOOLS

- Food processor
- Chopping board
- Sharp knife
- Scales
- Sieve
- Measuring jug
- Spoons
- Kitchen paper
- Garlic press

TIP

Any leftovers can be kept in a sealed container in the fridge for up to 4 days, or they can be frozen – make sure the purée is defrosted completely before serving.

INGREDIENTS

- 460g (1lb) jar roasted red peppers, drained and patted dry
- 1 small garlic clove, crushed
- 100g (3½oz) stale crusty bread
- ¼ tsp paprika, plus extra to serve
- ¼ tsp caster sugar
- 100g (3½oz) toasted flaked almonds
- ¾ tbsp sherry vinegar
- 90ml (3fl oz) extra virgin olive oil, plus extra to drizzle

TO SERVE
- Vegetable sticks
- Cucumber, diced
- Radishes, diced
- Handful of basil leaves
- Crackers

CHANGE IT UP!
As well as a dip and spread, this is a lovely paste to add to grilled chicken or fish.

1 ⚠ Put the peppers, garlic, bread, paprika, sugar, almonds, and vinegar in the food processor with a good pinch of salt. Whizz until it reaches a creamy paste texture.

2 ⚠ Slowly pour in the olive oil and whizz until the mixture is smooth and thick.

3 If you're using it as a dip, scrape the purée into a serving bowl. Use the back of a teaspoon to create a swirl on the surface. Drizzle over a little more olive oil and a sprinkle of paprika. Serve with your choice of vegetables.

4 If you're topping crackers, spread a little of the pepper purée on top of the cracker, then scatter over some finely diced cucumber and radishes and some small basil leaves. Eat right away so the crackers don't go soggy!

30 mins, plus draining

Serves 4

DUKKAH AND LABNEH

Dukkah is a finely crushed mix of spices, nuts, and salt that comes from Egypt. It's a tasty snack when combined with creamy labneh, which is strained yogurt. Dukkah can also be used to season meat.

TOOLS

- Spoons
- Scales
- Muslin cloth, or finely woven tea towel
- Kitchen string
- Kitchen scissors
- Pestle and mortar
- Mixing bowl
- Sieve
- Serving bowls
- Jar with lid

INGREDIENTS

FOR THE DUKKAH

- 40g (1½oz) roasted chopped hazelnuts
- 40g (1½oz) toasted flaked almonds
- 2 tsp cumin seeds
- 1 tsp ground coriander
- 2 tbsp sesame seeds
- 1 tsp sea salt flakes

FOR THE LABNEH

- 500g (1lb 2oz) full-fat Greek yogurt
- 2 large pinches of salt

TO SERVE

- Bread
- Olive oil
- Vegetables

 1 To make the dukkah, put all of the ingredients in the pestle and mortar. Pound them for a few minutes, until quite finely ground. Transfer to a serving bowl or a jar – the dukkah will keep for up to 3 weeks in an airtight container.

DUKKAH

A sprinkle of dukkah will give the Nectarine and feta salad on pp. 32—33 an extra crunch!

66

TO SERVE

Spread the labneh on some bread, sprinkle the dukkah over the top, and drizzle with some olive oil.

LABNEH

Chop up some vegetables to dip into the labneh then dukkah.

1 To make the labneh, open the yogurt, pour away any liquid that has gathered on the top, add the salt, and stir through.

2  Lay the cloth flat, then scoop the yogurt into the middle of it. Gather the four corners of cloth, and tie tightly with string to make a bag shape.

3  Put the bag in a sieve set over a mixing bowl. The excess liquid will drip away. Leave it in the fridge, still in the sieve over the mixing bowl for 24 hours before unwrapping.

4 Scoop the labneh into a serving bowl – it should be thick and creamy. Eat right away, or cover and keep in the fridge – it will stay fresh for up to 4 days.

ALMOND BUTTER DIP

This is a nutty and sweet alternative to savoury dips. It's easy to make as a snack or to pack in a lunchbox.

CHANGE IT UP!
You can substitute almond butter with the same amount of peanut butter.

15 mins,
plus soaking

Serves 4

TOOLS

- Spoons
- Mixing bowl
- Sieve
- Small food processor
- Serving bowl

INGREDIENTS

- 5 medjool dates, stones removed
- 4 tbsp almond butter
- 2 tbsp natural Greek yogurt
- ½ tsp vanilla extract
- Squeeze of lemon juice
- Roasted chopped hazelnuts, to garnish
- Sliced apples and pears, to serve
- Strawberries, to serve

TIP

Leftovers can be kept covered in the fridge for up to 1 week. Dollop over muesli, spread on toast, or add to smoothies!

1 Put the dates in the mixing bowl and cover with cold water. Leave to soak and soften for up to 30 minutes.

2 Take out 1 tbsp of the water and set aside, then drain the dates using the sieve.

3 ⚠ Put the dates, the water you set aside, and all of the remaining dip ingredients, except for the hazelnuts, in the small food processor. Whizz until completely smooth.

4 Scoop into a serving bowl, scatter over some chopped hazelnuts, and serve with fresh fruit for dipping.

SOAKED OLIVES

Plain olives can become a really yummy snack, just by letting them sit and soak up the flavours of other ingredients.

10 mins, plus marinating

Each recipe makes 200g (7oz)

TOOLS

- Chopping board
- Sharp knife
- Spoons
- Scales
- Airtight containers

LEMON AND FETA

INGREDIENTS

- 1–2 preserved lemons
- 60g (2oz) feta cheese
- 2 tsp cumin seeds
- 150g (5½oz) pitted black olives
- 4 tbsp olive oil

1 ⚠️ Slice each lemon in half and then into quarters. Carefully cut the flesh away from the lemon peel and throw away. Slice the peel into thin strips.

2 ⚠️ Roughly chop the feta cheese into chunks.

3 Put the feta cheese, lemon peel, and the rest of the ingredients in an airtight container. Stir together, then leave covered in the fridge for at least 6 hours before tucking in.

INGREDIENTS

HERB AND FENNEL

- 2 sprigs of rosemary, leaves picked
- 4 sprigs of thyme, leaves picked
- 2 tsp fennel seeds
- 150g (5½oz) pitted mixed green and black olives
- 4 tbsp olive oil

1 Mix all the ingredients together in an airtight container. Stir well, then leave to sit and soak in the fridge for at least 6 hours before you dive in.

TIP

All of these will keep for up to 2 days in an airtight container in the fridge. Once you eat the olives, you can use the leftover oil in salad dressings.

GARLIC AND CHILLI

INGREDIENTS

- 6 garlic cloves
- 1 tsp dried oregano
- Small pinch of chilli flakes
- 150g (5½oz) pitted green olives
- 4 tbsp olive oil

1 See p. 18 for how to peel the garlic cloves. Put the peeled garlic in an airtight container with the other ingredients and stir.

2 Keep covered in the fridge for at least 6 hours to help the flavours infuse together. Serve with a big pinch of pepper.

Grow in a
cool place

Plant
in spring

GROW YOUR OWN
SPINACH

This plant's green leaves and stalks are full of vitamins and minerals. Spinach helps you stay healthy and grow big and strong.

1 Fill the long container with compost. Use the ruler to make a trench about 2.5 cm (1 in) deep all along the compost. Sprinkle the spinach seeds in the trench, then cover with more compost.

2 As the spinach grows, remove some leaves to thin the plants out a bit – there should be a gap of roughly 8 cm (3 in) between each plant.

3 Water often, and use the liquid fertilizer once a month. Trim any small shoots when they grow from the larger leaves.

4 ⚠ When any leaves get longer than 5 cm (2 in), cut them off to wash and then eat!

TIP
Use your spinach in these recipes.

Spinach pesto courgetti p. 81

Couscous and spinach salad pp. 52–53

Green goodness smoothie p. 24

You can substitute the same amount of smoked trout for the mackerel.

TIP

Both the pâté and beetroot slaw can be made one day ahead of serving, just keep them covered in the fridge.

SMOKED FISH PÂTÉ

~~~~~~~~~~~~~~~~~~~~~~~~~~~~~~~

Pâté, meaning "paste", is a French dish often made from ground meat. This one, though, is made from smoky, salty fish.

20 mins, plus marinating

Serves 2–3

 1 To make the slaw, carefully grate the beetroot into a mixing bowl. Stir through the remaining ingredients until everything is combined. Set aside to marinate (soak together) for up to 30 minutes.

 2 To make the pâté, peel the skin off the mackerel fillets. Use your hands to break the fillets up into pieces and pop in a mixing bowl.

 3 Add the soured cream and lemon juice to the mackerel and mash with a fork until there are no big bits of fish left. Mash until everything is mixed together well.

 4 Stir in the parsley, then either scoop the pâté into ramekins, or pop large spoonfuls onto plates.

 5 Drain the slaw in a sieve to get rid of any extra liquid. Divide between the plates, then serve with crackers and enjoy!

TOOLS

- Mixing bowls
- Box grater
- Spoons
- Scales
- Fork
- Sharp knife
- Chopping board
- Vegetable peeler
- Sieve
- Ramekins or plates

INGREDIENTS

FOR THE BEETROOT SLAW

- 200g (7oz) raw beetroot, peeled and tops trimmed
- Juice of ½ a lemon
- 1 tsp caster sugar
- Large pinch of salt
- ½ tbsp olive oil

FOR THE PÂTÉ

- 230g (8oz) boneless smoked mackerel
- 50g (1¾oz) soured cream
- Squeeze of lemon juice
- 15g (½oz) parsley, roughly chopped
- Crackers, to serve

SHRIMP
BUTTER POTS

Before fridges were invented, mixing shrimps with butter was one way to keep them from going off. It's also a very tasty way to eat them – especially when the butter is flavoured with herbs, spices, and lemon.

30 mins, plus chilling

Serves 4

TOOLS

- Electric whisk
- Scales
- Measuring jug
- 4 ramekins or small jars each with 100ml (3½fl oz) capacity
- Mixing bowls
- Sieve
- Microplane
- Vegetable peeler
- Cling film
- Spoons

INGREDIENTS

- 150g (5½oz) unsalted butter
- Large pinch of cayenne powder
- Large pinch of ground mace
- Zest of ½ a lemon
- 10g (¼oz) chives, finely chopped
- 140g (5oz) pre-cooked brown shrimps, drained
- Crusty brown bread, to serve

FOR THE PICKLED CUCUMBER

- ½ a cucumber
- 50ml (2fl oz) white wine vinegar
- 15g (½oz) caster sugar
- ¼ tsp fine salt

TIP

If you don't have ground mace, you can use ground nutmeg.

1. Leave the butter out at room temperature for a few hours until it's really soft when you prod it. Pop in a mixing bowl.

2. ⚠ Add the cayenne powder, ground mace, lemon zest, chives, and a large pinch of salt to the bowl. Whisk with the electric whisk for 1–2 minutes, or until the mixture turns a pale colour and has a soft, fluffy texture.

3. Stir in the brown shrimp using a spoon. Once everything is mixed together, divide between the ramekins or jars. Cover with cling film, and leave in the fridge overnight.

4. The next day, take the shrimp pots out of the fridge about 30 minutes before serving so that the mixture can soften. Meanwhile, use the vegetable peeler to peel ribbons of cucumber.

5. Put the cucumber in a mixing bowl with the vinegar, sugar, and salt and toss to coat. Leave to stand for 20 minutes, stirring halfway through.

6. Once the ribbons have softened, drain in a sieve and gently squeeze to get rid of any extra liquid.

TO SERVE

Serve the shrimp pots with a handful of pickled cucumbers and some brown crusty bread. The shrimp pots will keep covered in the fridge for up to 3 days.

COURGETTI

Using a spiralizer will give you courgette strands that look very similar to spaghetti. But unlike spaghetti, courgetti doesn't need to be cooked – just add a tasty sauce and enjoy a healthy dinner.

20 mins   Serves 4

TOOLS

- Chopping board
- Sharp knife
- Spiralizer
- Scissors

FOR THE COURGETTI BASE

- 4 courgettes, halved with bases trimmed

1 See p. 14 for how to use a spiralizer. Use it to cut the courgette – you should end up with a big tangle of courgetti. Repeat for the remaining courgettes.

2 If the strands are longer than normal spaghetti, use scissors to trim them down. Use the courgetti as soon as you've spiralized it – it doesn't keep very well and can become soft.

3 Choose one of the three sauces on this page or the next, coat the courgetti, twirl it around your fork, and enjoy!

CHANGE IT UP!

If you don't have a spiralizer, a julienne peeler is a great alternative, and will produce lovely courgette strands.

CREAMY AVOCADO AND PARMESAN

5 mins

Serves 4

TOOLS

- Chopping board
- Sharp knife
- Food processor
- Mixing bowl
- Scales
- Garlic press
- Microplane
- Spoons

TO SERVE
- Small mint leaves
- Sprinkle of chilli flakes

INGREDIENTS

- 2 ripe avocados
- 40g (1½oz) Parmesan cheese, grated, plus extra to serve
- Juice of 1 lemon, plus the grated zest to serve
- 1 garlic clove, crushed
- 2 tbsp extra virgin olive oil, plus extra to serve
- Courgetti base

1 See p. 14 for how to cut open an avocado and remove the stone. Repeat for the second avocado.

2 Using a spoon, scoop the flesh out from each avocado half, then put it in the food processor. Add the Parmesan cheese, lemon juice, crushed garlic, olive oil, and a pinch of salt.

3 Whizz everything until it's completely smooth, then taste and add more salt if you think it needs it.

4 Put the courgetti base in a bowl and pour over the sauce. Using your hands, toss everything together until the courgetti is completely coated in the sauce. It might be messy work, but it's worth it!

5 Divide between 4 bowls. Top with some lemon zest, a few mint leaves, chilli flakes if you can handle the spice, and finally a drizzle of olive oil.

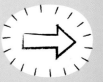

10 mins, plus marinating

Serves 4

TOOLS

- Chopping board
- Sharp knife
- Mixing bowl
- Spoons
- Scales

INGREDIENTS

- 120g (4oz) feta cheese
- 500g (1lb 2oz) tomatoes, roughly chopped
- 2 tsp red wine vinegar
- Large pinch of caster sugar
- 2 tbsp extra virgin olive oil, plus extra to serve
- Courgetti base (p. 78)
- 1 tsp dried oregano

 1 Use your hands to break the feta cheese into chunks and set aside. Pop the tomatoes, vinegar, sugar, olive oil, and a pinch of salt in the mixing bowl.

 2 Stir everything together, then leave to soak for 15–20 minutes so that the tomatoes soften and release tasty juices into the bowl.

 3 Pop the courgetti base into the mixing bowl, and toss together with the tomato mixture. Stir through the feta cheese chunks and oregano. Divide between 4 bowls, then twist it up and eat!

SIMPLE TOMATO

80

SPINACH PESTO

10 mins   Serves 4

TOOLS

- Food processor
- Mixing bowl
- Spoons
- Scales
- Garlic press

INGREDIENTS

- 100g (3½oz) spinach leaves
- 40g (1½oz) fresh basil leaves, plus extra to serve
- 60g (2oz) pine nuts
- 1 garlic clove, crushed
- 3 tbsp olive oil
- 50g (1¾oz) Parmesan cheese, grated, plus extra to serve
- Courgetti base (p. 78)

1 ⚠ Put all of the ingredients, apart from the courgetti base, into the food processor with a generous helping of salt and pepper. Whizz until the pesto is smooth.

2 Place the courgetti base in the mixing bowl and spoon in the pesto. Use your hands to coat the courgetti.

3 Divide between 4 bowls and top with some basil leaves and a little more grated Parmesan – add as much as you like.

30 mins Makes 5

PRAWN SUMMER ROLLS

These mouth-watering rolls are inspired by Vietnamese flavours and are filled with fresh vegetables, herbs, and prawns. They are both fun to make and scrumptious to eat!

INGREDIENTS

- 1 carrot, peeled
- ⅓ cucumber
- 5 little gem lettuce leaves
- 5 rice paper wrappers
- 150g (5½oz) pre-cooked king prawns
- 20 mint leaves
- 2 spring onions, thinly sliced lengthways

TOOLS

- Julienne peeler
- Scales
- Frying pan
- Spoons
- Mixing bowl
- Chopping board
- Tea towel
- Scissors
- Garlic press

FOR THE DIPPING SAUCE

- 3 tbsp peanut butter
- 1 tsp soy sauce
- 2 tsp fish sauce
- 1 tsp caster sugar
- Juice of ½ a lime
- ½ garlic clove, crushed
- 2 tbsp water

Don't forget to dip the rolls in the sauce!

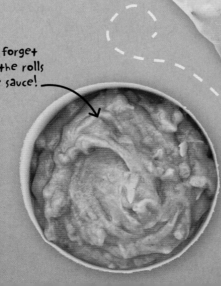

82

1 Carefully drag the julienne peeler down the length of each side of the carrot so you get lots of little strands. Stop when you reach the carrot's core.

 2 Repeat with the cucumber, stopping when you reach the seeds. Snip the lettuce leaves into thin slices.

3 Divide the vegetables into 5 piles, each with slices of carrot, cucumber, and lettuce. Stir all of the sauce ingredients together and set aside.

 4 Fill a frying pan with cold water. Dip a rice paper wrapper into it for 1–2 minutes, until it goes completely floppy.

5 Once the wrapper is soft, lift it out of the pan very carefully – try not to let it fold in on itself. Gently lay it down on a clean tea towel.

 These summer rolls will keep in the fridge, wrapped in cling film, for 1 day.

 6 Line up 4 prawns across the middle of the wrapper, then top with 4 mint leaves, some spring onion, and one of the vegetable piles.

7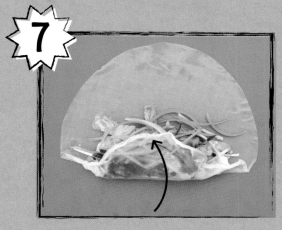

Carefully cover the filling with the bottom of the wrapper.

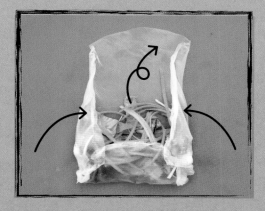

Fold both sides of the wrapper inwards. Finally, gently roll it all up as tightly as you can.

 8 Transfer to a plate. Repeat steps 4–7 until you have 5 rolls in total. Serve with the dipping sauce.

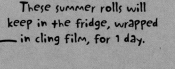

83

COLESLAW THREE WAYS

20 mins, plus marinating

Each recipe serves 4

Coleslaw is made with cabbage, carrot, and onion. Try adding the extra ingredients here for different flavours or choose your own!

INGREDIENTS

- ¼ white cabbage, finely chopped
- 1 large carrot, grated
- ½ red onion, thinly sliced

TOOLS

- Chopping board
- Sharp knife
- Mixing bowl
- Spoons
- Box grater

This coleslaw is yummy at barbecues.

CLASSIC COLESLAW

1 To make the coleslaw base, put the white cabbage, carrot, and red onion in the mixing bowl. Stir in the extra ingredients needed for whichever coleslaw you choose to make.

2 Cover and chill for at least 30 minutes, or overnight, so the flavours can soak into the vegetables.

INGREDIENTS

- 1 tbsp mayonnaise
- 1 tbsp full-fat natural yogurt
- Squeeze of lemon juice

1 Mix everything together in a bowl with some salt, then pour over the coleslaw base and toss until coated.

TIP

If you have a julienne attachment on your food processor, you can use that to thinly slice the vegetables instead of slicing by hand.

APPLE COLESLAW

This coleslaw is delicious when eaten with slices of cheese and cooked ham.

SESAME COLESLAW

This tangy coleslaw goes well with the Chicken and mango boats on pp. 94–95, or the Prawn summer rolls on pp. 82–83.

INGREDIENTS

- 1 apple
- 4 sprigs of parsley, leaves finely chopped
- 1 tbsp wholegrain mustard
- 2 tsp red wine vinegar

INGREDIENTS

- 1 tbsp toasted sesame oil
- 2 tbsp sesame seeds
- Juice of 1–2 limes

1 Use a sharp knife to carefully cut down each side of the apple, until you're left with four large pieces and the core. Cut each piece into thin strips, and throw away the core.

1 Mix all of the ingredients together in a bowl and add a pinch of salt. Pour over and coat the coleslaw base.

2 Mix the apple and parsley through the coleslaw base, then stir in the mustard, red wine vinegar, and a pinch of salt. Toss until coated.

Keep any leftover sauce in a sealed jar in the fridge for up to 5 days.

TIP
If you're not sure about the mustard flavour, add half of the mustard first, then the rest at the end if you like it.

SWEET MUSTARD AND DILL SAUCE

15 mins

Serves 4

This sweet and sharp sauce is creamy and pairs perfectly with smoked salmon. Enjoy at breakfast, lunch, or dinner!

TOOLS

- Spoons
- Scales
- Whisk
- Mixing bowl
- Measuring jug
- Scissors

INGREDIENTS

- 1 egg yolk
- 1 tbsp white wine vinegar
- 1 tbsp Dijon mustard
- ½ tbsp caster sugar
- 150ml (5fl oz) sunflower oil
- 10g (¼oz) fresh dill, finely snipped
- Juice of ½ a lemon

TO SERVE

- 4 slices of brown bread, buttered and cut into triangles
- 200g (7oz) smoked salmon
- Lemon wedges

Please note: the finished recipe contains uncooked egg.

1 Put the egg yolk, vinegar, mustard, and sugar in a medium mixing bowl with a large pinch of salt. Whisk for 1–2 minutes until everything is combined and has a pale colour.

2

Slowly pour in the oil while continuously whisking. (You could ask someone to pour while you mix.) The mixture should thicken up a little.

Make sure you add the oil in a slow stream, not all at once.

3 Once all the oil has been mixed in, stir in the dill and then taste the sauce. If it needs a bit more sharpness, squeeze in some lemon juice.

4 Arrange the bread triangles and smoked salmon on 4 plates. Drizzle the sauce over the salmon and serve with lemon wedges.

PANZANELLA

This salad comes from Italy and is an excellent way to use up any stale bread you have, such as the leftover bread from the Muffuletta on pp. 30–31. The juices from the tomatoes and peppers soak into the bread, making it soft and chewy.

30 mins, plus soaking

Serves 4

TOOLS

- Chopping board
- Sharp knife
- Mixing bowl
- Spoons
- Scales
- Salad servers

INGREDIENTS

- 2 red peppers
- 1kg (2¼lb) ripe tomatoes
- 3 tbsp capers
- 4 tsp red wine vinegar
- 4 tbsp extra virgin olive oil, plus extra for drizzling
- ½ tsp caster sugar
- 300g (10oz) very stale bread
- 2 handfuls of basil leaves
- 2 medium-sized balls mozzarella cheese

 1 Carefully slice the four sides off each red pepper and throw away the leftover seeds and stalk. Cut away any white bits from inside the pepper pieces. Chop the peppers into rough chunks.

 2 Roughly chop the tomatoes. They should be a similar size to the chunks of red pepper.

 3 Put the peppers, tomatoes, and capers in the mixing bowl. Scatter over a pinch of salt, then set aside for about 10 minutes – the juices will start to come out of the tomatoes.

 4 Mix together the vinegar, olive oil, and sugar. Pour this mixture over the tomatoes, peppers, and capers, then toss everything together with the salad servers.

5 Tear the bread into pieces, then stir it into the mixing bowl. Allow the panzanella to sit for about 20–30 minutes, giving it a stir every now and then, until the bread is soft and has soaked up the juices.

6 Stir through the basil leaves, then divide between 4 bowls. Tear each mozzarella ball in half, then place in each bowl. Drizzle with a little more olive oil. Add a pinch of salt and pepper, then tuck in!

TACO FEAST

These make-your-own tacos are full of different flavours. Put all of the dishes on the table so that everyone can choose their favourites.

FOR THE SMASHED AVOCADO

- 2 ripe avocados
- Juice of ½ a lime, plus extra to taste
- 30g (1oz) bunch of coriander

1 See p. 14 for how to cut open an avocado and remove the stone. Repeat for the second avocado.

2 Use a spoon to scoop the flesh out from each avocado half. Put this in a mixing bowl with the lime juice and a pinch of salt.

3 Snip the coriander stalks into the bowl. Set aside the leaves (you'll need them for the sweetcorn salsa!). Mash together, then taste. If you think it needs a little more sharpness, squeeze in some extra lime juice.

FOR THE CHICKEN

- 2 pre-cooked chicken breasts, shredded
- 4 medium tomatoes, diced
- 1 tsp ground cumin
- ¼ tsp paprika
- ¼ tsp ground coriander
- 1 tsp dried oregano
- Drizzle of olive oil
- 30g (1oz) bunch of coriander, roughly chopped

1 Mix all of the ingredients together, then season generously with salt and pepper.

TO SERVE

Get out the soured cream, grated cheese, lime wedges, and tacos. Give everyone a plate then wrap up your tacos!

Smashed avocado

Soured cream

Chicken

40 mins

Serves 4

TOOLS

- Small food processor
- Scales
- Chopping board
- Sharp knife
- Scissors
- Spoons
- Mixing bowls
- Can opener
- Sieve
- Garlic press

TO SERVE

- Soured cream
- Grated cheese of your choice
- Lime wedges
- Soft corn tacos

FOR THE BEAN DIP

- 400g (14oz) can of red kidney beans, drained
- 3 tbsp olive oil
- 1 garlic clove, crushed
- ½ tsp ground cumin
- ¼ tsp ground cinnamon
- Juice of ½ a lemon
- Pinch of paprika, plus extra to serve

1 Put all of the ingredients in a small food processor with 3 tbsp water and whizz until smooth.

2 Season with salt and pepper, then scoop into a serving bowl and sprinkle over some paprika.

FOR THE SWEETCORN SALSA

- ½ red onion, finely chopped
- Juice of 2 limes
- 1 tsp caster sugar
- 1 red pepper, finely chopped and deseeded
- 200g (7oz) can of sweetcorn, drained

1 Mix the onion with lime juice, a pinch of salt, and the sugar in a mixing bowl. Set aside for 10 minutes to soak, then add the rest of the ingredients.

2 Roughly chop the coriander leaves you set aside to make the smashed avocado. Stir the leaves through the sweetcorn salsa.

3 Season with another pinch of salt, then pop on the table and start building your tacos.

Don't forget about your favourite cheese!

Bean dip

Sweetcorn salsa

Wrap everything together in soft corn tacos.

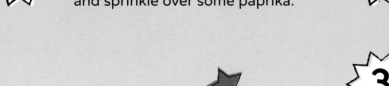

SEAFOOD HANDROLLS

Japanese handrolls are often filled with rice and other ingredients, but you can also make them with just vegetables and seafood sticks. Roll them the right way, and you *should* be able to eat them with one hand!

 1 Start by preparing your vegetables. Carefully cut the cucumber in half lengthways, then use a teaspoon to scrape out the seeds. Cut into long, thin batons and set aside.

 2 Carefully slice the 4 sides off the red pepper and discard the seeds and stalk. Cut away any white bits from inside the pepper pieces, then slice into long, thin batons.

 3 Trim the root off the lettuce and gently pull the leaves off. Cut the leaves lengthways into thin strips. Pop the cucumber, pepper, lettuce, and beansprouts on a plate.

 4 Take a nori sheet and lay it flat on a clean, dry surface. The smooth side of the nori sheet should be facing downwards.

CHANGE IT UP!
To make this vegetarian, swap the seafood sticks for avocado slices.

25 mins

Makes 5

TOOLS

- Sharp knife
- Chopping board
- Table knife
- Spoons
- Plate

INGREDIENTS

- ⅓ cucumber
- 1 red pepper
- 1 little gem lettuce
- Handful of beansprouts
- 10 seafood sticks
- 5 chives
- 5 rectangular nori (seaweed) sheets

TO SERVE
- Black or white sesame seeds
- Juice of ½ a lime
- Sweet chilli sauce, to drizzle

5

When rolling, start from the bottom left-hand corner.

Place one-fifth of the vegetables on the left-hand side of the nori, arranged diagonally. Put 2 seafood sticks and a chive folded in half on top.

6

Dampen this edge.

Roll the nori around the filling so it forms a cone. Once rolled, wet your fingers and dampen the nori – stick it to the cone to secure the roll. Repeat to make 4 more handrolls.

To serve, scatter some sesame seeds and squeeze some lime juice over the filling. Drizzle with sweet chilli sauce.

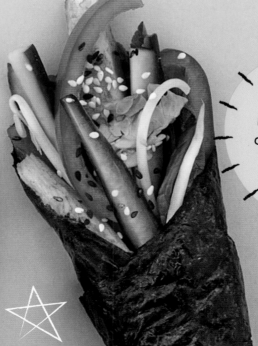

DID YOU KNOW?
Nori is a type of edible seaweed often used in Japanese cooking. The seaweed is pounded into sheets, and then dried.

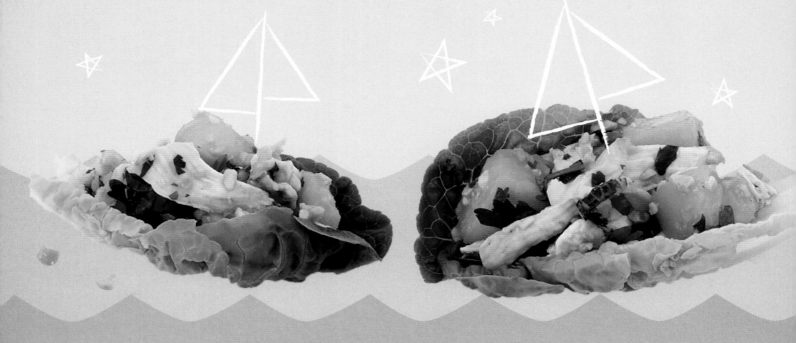

CHICKEN AND MANGO BOATS

Lettuce leaves are great for holding fillings. They are also easy to roll up and eat. These crunchy salad bites are full of flavour – they are sweet, sour, salty, and a little bit spicy!

INGREDIENTS

- 50g (1¾oz) salted peanuts
- 1 ripe mango
- 2 pre-cooked chicken breasts, shredded
- Juice of 1 lime
- 3 mint sprigs, roughly chopped
- 15g (½oz) coriander leaves, roughly chopped
- 2 tbsp sweet chilli sauce
- 1 tsp fish sauce
- 1–2 little gem lettuces

TOOLS

- Pestle and mortar
- Sharp knife
- Chopping board
- Table knife
- Spoons
- Scales
- Mixing bowls

20 mins

Makes 16

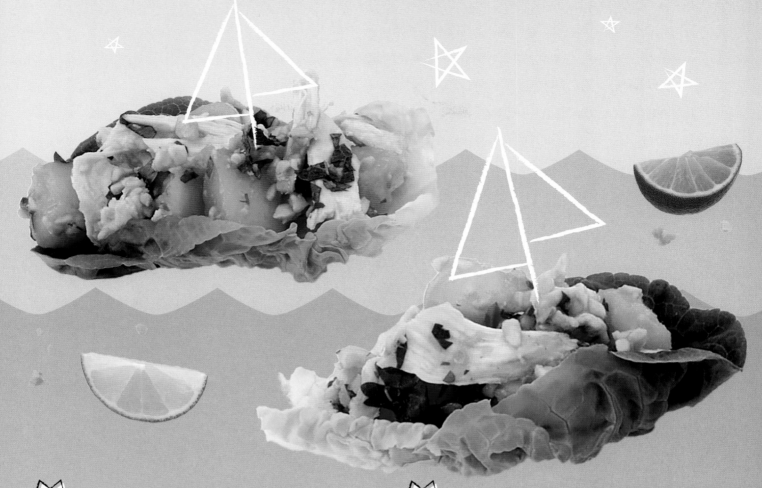

1 ⚠
Put the peanuts in the pestle and mortar, and grind them up until they're finely crushed. Carefully cut down the sides of the mango, avoiding the stone.

2 ⚠

Once scored, your mango should have lots of little squares on it.

Lay the cut mango skin side down on the chopping board. Use the table knife to score thin lines down and across the flesh, stopping when you reach the skin.

3
Use a spoon to scoop the flesh out. The mango will be in small cubes. Pop them in a bowl with the peanuts and shredded chicken, then mix it all up. Stir in the rest of the ingredients, except the lettuce.

4 ⚠
Trim the root off the lettuce, then gently pull the leaves off one by one, trimming more off the root when needed. You'll need 16 leaves in total. Divide the filling between the lettuce boats and you're done!

RAW PIZZA

This recipe has all of the flavours of a pizza, without any of the cooking! We've topped ours with slices of pepperoni, mozzarella cheese, and fresh tomatoes, but you can get creative and use whatever toppings you like.

 15 mins

 Makes 4

TIP

Use flatbreads for this recipe, not pre-made pizza bases.

TOOLS

- Mini food processor
- Scales
- Chopping board
- Pizza cutter
- Spoons

INGREDIENTS

- 4 flatbreads

FOR THE SAUCE

- 180g (6oz) sunblush tomatoes, drained
- 35g (1oz) mascarpone
- Handful of basil leaves, plus extra to serve

TO TOP EACH PIZZA

- 5 slices of pepperoni
- 6 mini mozzarella cheese balls, halved
- 3 cherry tomatoes, halved

CHANGE IT UP!

You can also use the sauce to make pizza wraps! Spread 1 tbsp of the sauce on a soft tortilla wrap. Add the pizza toppings, then roll up the wrap. Any remaining sauce will keep covered in the fridge for up to 1 week. This sauce is also delicious stirred through cooked pasta, or as a dip with breadsticks and vegetables.

1 ⚠️ To make the sauce, put the sunblush tomatoes, mascarpone, and basil in the mini food processor. Whizz until you have a smooth sauce.

2 Spoon 2 tbsp of the sauce onto each flatbread. Use the back of the spoon to spread the sauce out – make sure you leave a small gap around the edges so you have a crust!

3 Top with pepperoni slices, mozzarella cheese, tomatoes, and the extra basil leaves.

4 ⚠️ To serve, use the pizza cutter to cut each flatbread into quarters. Fold each quarter in half and dig in using your hands!

COURGETTE AND TUNA SALAD

This salad has a creamy dressing and is packed with loads of flavour. The butter beans make it really filling, so you could have it on its own for lunch or dinner.

TOOLS

- Vegetable peeler
- Sharp knife
- Can opener
- Chopping board
- Sieve
- Mixing bowls
- Spoons
- Scales
- Bowls

20 mins, plus marinating

Serves 3–4

INGREDIENTS

- 1 large courgette
- Juice of ½ a lemon
- 400g (14oz) can of butter beans, drained and rinsed
- 100g (3½oz) radishes, thinly sliced
- 160g (6oz) can of tuna in brine, drained

FOR THE DRESSING

- 50g (1¾oz) crème fraîche
- Juice of ½ a lemon
- 10g (¼oz) chives, finely chopped
- 1 tsp olive oil

 Carefully slice both ends off the courgette, then drag the vegetable peeler lengthways along the courgette to make ribbons – stop when you get to the seeds (you can throw these away).

 Put the courgette ribbons in a bowl, squeeze over the lemon juice, and sprinkle over a pinch of salt. Use your hands to coat the courgette ribbons. Leave to soften for up to 10 minutes.

 Meanwhile, make the dressing by stirring all of the ingredients together in a bowl. Season with salt and pepper and set aside.

 Once the courgettes have softened, squeeze them gently to release any liquid. Remove the extra liquid from the bowl. Add the butter beans and sliced radishes. Pour in the dressing and toss everything together.

 Pop the tuna into the bowl, making sure to break up any large chunks. Give the salad a final stir – be gentle so you don't break the tuna up too much. Plate it up and tuck in!

Grow in a
sunny place

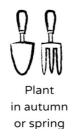

Plant
in autumn
or spring

GROW YOUR OWN
STRAWBERRIES

1 Fill the medium pot with soil. Leave a small hole in the middle of the soil. Put the strawberry plug in the hole, then cover the bottom of the plug with soil. Water well.

2

To stop the strawberries from touching the ground, add some straw to cover the soil. This will lift up your growing strawberries.

These bright red fruits should be planted somewhere where there is no wind. They will be ready to enjoy in the summer sunshine.

TOOLS

- Strawberry plug
- Medium pot
- Soil
- Straw
- Liquid fertilizer

3 This plant needs to be watered every day. Start giving it liquid fertilizer every 10 days once the strawberries start to grow.

4 Once any strawberries turn red, pick them right away. Keep the plant well watered to help the strawberries grow big and juicy. Wash before tucking in!

TIP
Use your strawberries in these recipes.

Berry and cherry oats P. 23

Eton mess semifreddo P. 123

FRUIT FOOLS

15 mins,
plus chilling

Makes 4

Nothing beats a creamy fruit fool on a hot day.
They can be made with whatever fruit you have
at home. We've used berries and plums, but you
can try out your own flavour combinations!

TOOLS

- Sharp knife
- Chopping board
- Scales
- Measuring jug
- Mixing bowl
- Spoons
- Sieve
- Electric whisk
- 4 serving glasses
- Cling film

INGREDIENTS

- 2 plums
- 150ml (5fl oz) double cream
- 200g (7oz) full-fat
  Greek yogurt
- 1 tsp vanilla extract
- 2 tbsp icing sugar
- 3 tbsp berry compote, or jam
- 2 ginger biscuits,
  to serve

1 Begin by preparing your plums. Using the sharp knife and the chopping board, carefully cut down each side of the plum, until you're left with 4 large pieces and the stone.

2 Cut each chunk into small pieces, and throw away the stone. Repeat for the other plum. Set aside.

3 Put the double cream, yogurt, and vanilla extract into the mixing bowl. Use the sieve to sift in the icing sugar.

4 Whisk the mixture for 1–2 minutes with the electric whisk until it forms soft, shiny peaks. Don't whip too much or it will become grainy. The peaks should flop over when you lift the whisk out.

5 Dollop 3 tablespoons of the berry compote into different places in the cream. Carefully fold the compote into the cream, until you have a swirled effect – don't stir it in completely.

6 Divide half of the plum pieces between 4 glasses, then pour in some of the cream. Top with the remaining plums, then the rest of the cream.

7 Chill in the fridge for up to 30 minutes. Cover with cling film if leaving in the fridge overnight. When ready to eat, crumble over the biscuits. Ta-dah!

CHOCOLATE POWER BALLS

These little chewy bites are excellent energy-boosting snacks between meals.

 30 mins, plus chilling

 Makes 14

TOOLS

- Food processor
- Plates
- Cling film
- Spoons
- Scales
- Pestle and mortar

INGREDIENTS

- 100g (3½oz) pecans
- 4 dates, stones removed
- 50g (1¾oz) desiccated coconut
- 3 tbsp almond butter, or other nut butter
- 4 tsp cocoa powder
- 1 tbsp maple syrup
- 1 tbsp vegetable oil
- 10g (¼oz) freeze-dried strawberries

 1 Put the pecans in the food processor and whizz until finely crushed.

 2 Pop the remaining ingredients, except for the freeze-dried strawberries, in the food processor. Whizz everything until it's smooth.

 3 Using your hands, roll the mixture up into small balls, then put on a plate – you should end up with 14 balls. Cover with cling film and chill for 1 hour.

 4 Finely crush the freeze-dried strawberries in the pestle and mortar – they should turn into a powder.

 5 Now decorate! Dip a ball into the strawberry powder so you coat half of it. Repeat for the remaining balls.

 6 Transfer your chocolate power balls to an airtight container and chill until you want one. These will keep in the fridge for up to 2 weeks, but are so tasty they might not last that long!

RASPBERRY RIPPLE FRIDGE CAKE

CHANGE IT UP!
You can choose any type of biscuit you'd like, flavour the cream with maple syrup or elderflower, and decorate with different toppings!

This is one of the easiest cakes you'll ever make. Take your time building up the biscuity tower, before demolishing the whole thing and tucking in!

25 mins, plus chilling

Serves 10–12

TOOLS

- Scales
- Mixing bowl
- Measuring jug
- Electric whisk
- Spoons
- Fork

INGREDIENTS

- 300ml (10fl oz) whipping cream
- 200g (7oz) full-fat Greek yogurt
- 2 tsp vanilla extract
- 3 tbsp icing sugar
- 225g (8oz) raspberries
- 15–20 jam-filled biscuits

1 Put the whipping cream, yogurt, vanilla extract, and icing sugar in a bowl. Whisk with the electric whisk for 2–3 minutes, until the mixture forms soft peaks. The mixture will flop over when you lift the whisk out.

2 Crush 100g (3½oz) of the raspberries in a bowl with a fork. Dollop them into the cream mixture, and gently fold together.

3 Put 6 biscuits in a circle on the serving plate, then place 1 more in the centre of the circle. Cover with some of the cream mixture.

Scatter some of the remaining raspberries between each layer of cream.

4 Arrange 4 more biscuits in a circle on top of the cream. Cover with more cream and raspberries.

5 Top with a triangle of 3 biscuits and cover with the remaining cream and raspberries.

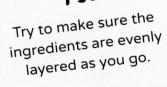

TIP

Try to make sure the ingredients are evenly layered as you go.

6 Balance the final biscuit on top, then transfer to the fridge for at least 30 minutes, or up to 12 hours.

MINI TRIFLES

The best thing about a trifle is the way it's made, with layer on layer of tasty filling. Choose your favourite flavours or mix-and-match.

10 mins, plus chilling

Each recipe makes 4

TOOLS

- Mixing bowls
- Scales
- Spoons
- Freezer bag
- Rolling pin
- Sharp knife
- Chopping board
- Serving glasses
- Can opener

TO SERVE

If eating right away, top each trifle with some spray cream, then finish with a sprinkle of the toppings. Or, don't add the toppings, cover, and keep in the fridge for up to 12 hours.

INGREDIENTS

- 250g (9oz) vanilla yogurt
- 4 tbsp chocolate spread
- 8 digestive biscuits
- 200g (7oz) raspberries
- Spray cream, to serve
- 4 tbsp mini marshmallows, to top

1 Put the yogurt in a mixing bowl and dollop over the chocolate spread. Swirl through the yogurt with a spoon, then set aside.

2 Crumble the biscuits into large pieces, then divide half of the biscuit pieces between 4 glasses.

3 Tear up the raspberries with your fingers, and divide half of them between the glasses. Top with the yogurt mixture, then the rest of the biscuit pieces and raspberries.

S'mores are biscuits filled with melted chocolate and marshmallows. They are often eaten around a campfire — this trifle has the flavour, but none of the fire!

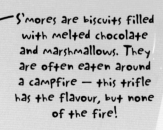

S'MORES

INGREDIENTS

- 8 ginger biscuits, plus crumbs to top
- 4 bananas, peeled and sliced
- 6 tbsp caramel sauce
- 250g (9oz) vanilla yogurt
- Spray cream, to serve

 Put the biscuits in the freezer bag. Close the bag, then bash gently with the rolling pin until the biscuits are roughly crushed.

 Divide half of the crushed biscuits between 4 glasses, then pop half of the banana slices in each glass.

 Pour the caramel sauce into each glass. Dollop the yogurt on top, then add the rest of the crushed biscuits and bananas.

Make sure your bananas are nice and ripe, with speckled skins.

BANOFFEE

INGREDIENTS

- 120g (4oz) sponge cake, crumbled into small pieces
- 12 peach slices from a can, roughly chopped, plus the juice
- 175g (6oz) pre-made strawberry jelly
- 300g (10oz) pre-made custard
- Spray cream, to serve
- Sweet popcorn, to top
- Sprinkles, to top

 Divide the cake pieces between 4 glasses and press down on them with your fingers. Pour 1 tbsp of the peach juice into each glass for the cake to soak up.

 Divide the chopped peaches between the glasses. Top with the jelly and custard.

This trifle is full of fruit, jelly, and custard. We've topped it with crunchy popcorn and sprinkles!

PEACHES AND CREAM

WATERMELON SLUSH

**15 mins,
plus freezing**

Makes 4

This ice-cold drink is zingy and fruity. It's easy to make and you can swap out the watermelon for other melon if you like.

TOOLS

• Blender
• 1.2 litre (2 pint) freezer-proof container
• Fork
• 4 glasses
• Scales
• Spoons
• Paper straws, lime wedges, and cocktail umbrellas (optional)

INGREDIENTS

• 900g (2lb) watermelon, peeled carefully, cut into quarters, deseeded and cut into chunks (see p. 7 "Kitchen safety" for how to cut a large fruit with a thick skin)
• 1 tbsp caster sugar
• Juice of 1 lime

 1 Put all of the ingredients in the blender and whizz until the mixture is a smooth juice. Pour into the freezer-proof container and freeze for 1–2 hours.

 2 After 1–2 hours, remove from the freezer and scrape the fork through the mixture, breaking up any bits that have frozen solid.

 3 Put the container back in the freezer and repeat step 2 each hour for the next 4–5 hours, or until the mixture becomes a frozen slush.

 4 When you want to dig in, allow the slush to melt at room temperature for 5–10 minutes. Pour into glasses and decorate with colourful straws, lime wedges, and tiny umbrellas, if you like.

CHANGE IT UP!
You can use cantaloupe or honeydew melon instead, but add a splash of water when blending.

BLACK FOREST
BANANA SPLITS

If you can't get frozen cherries, try frozen summer fruits instead.

Inspired by the chocolate and cherry flavours of a Black Forest gateau, these banana splits are made with instant ice cream. Add yogurt to frozen fruit and watch it magically transform before your eyes!

20 mins, plus freezing

Makes 4

TOOLS

- Scales
- Spoons
- Food processor
- Freezer-proof container
- Ice cream scoop
- Table knife
- Bowl
- Chopping board

INGREDIENTS

- 400g (14oz) frozen cherries, stones removed
- 250g (9oz) full-fat Greek yogurt
- 2 tbsp golden syrup
- 4 bananas
- Spray cream
- 12 fresh cherries
- Chocolate sauce and sprinkles, to serve

1 To make the ice cream, put the frozen cherries, yogurt, and golden syrup in the food processor. Whizz until it reaches a smooth ice cream texture.

2 Pour the mixture into a freezer-proof container and freeze for at least 2½ hours.

3 When ready to serve, take the ice cream out of the freezer. If it's too solid, leave it out at room temperature to soften a little.

4 Meanwhile, peel then carefully slice the bananas in half lengthways. Place 2 halves in a bowl, then top with 2 scoops of ice cream, some spray cream, 3 fresh cherries, a drizzle of chocolate sauce, and a scatter of sprinkles.

TIP

You can keep any leftover ice cream covered in the freezer for up to 1 week.

113

APPLE DOUGHNUTS

30 mins

Makes 8

There's no dough in these "doughnuts" – just lots of fresh fruit and crunchy nuts.

INGREDIENTS

- 2 apples
- 4 tsp peanut butter, or other nut butter spread
- 4 tsp chocolate spread

TO TOP

- Dried fruit, such as raisins or chopped apricots
- Sprinkles (chocolate or multi-coloured)
- Freeze-dried raspberries or strawberries, roughly crushed
- Chopped nuts, such as hazelnuts or pecans
- Desiccated coconut

TOOLS

- Sharp knife
- Chopping board
- Apple corer
- Kitchen paper
- Spoons

This one is topped with peanut butter and sprinkles. Yum!

Get creative with toppings! You can use anything you like.

1 ⚠️ Carefully cut the top and bottom off each apple, then use the apple corer to remove both cores.

2 ⚠️ Cut each apple horizontally into 4 pieces, so that you end up with 4 rings per apple. Use kitchen paper to blot each ring to dry its surface a little.

3 Spread peanut butter on 4 rings and chocolate spread on the other 4. Scatter over toppings of your choice, then chomp away!

NO-BAKE CRUMBLES

 10 mins **Makes 6 crumble bases**

Serve these fruity crumbles with custard or ice cream. You can mix and match fillings and toppings to find the combinations you like best.

TIP
The crumble base will keep in an airtight container somewhere cool and dry for up to 5 days.

TOOLS

- Scales
- Food processor
- Spoons
- Airtight container

FOR THE CRUMBLE BASE

- 50g (1¾oz) speculoos biscuits, or other spiced biscuits
- 25g (1oz) pretzels
- 100g (3½oz) low-sugar granola
- 40g (1½oz) maple syrup

 1 ⚠ Put the biscuits, pretzels, and granola into the food processor. Whizz until everything is quite finely crushed, but has a breadcrumb-like texture.

 2 Divide your choice of filling between 6 bowls. Stir the maple syrup through the crumble topping just before you add it to the fruit, to stop it going soggy.

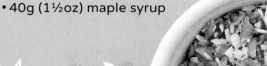

25 mins, plus soaking

Makes 6

PLUM AND RASPBERRY

TOOLS

- Box grater
- Spoons
- Scales
- Mixing bowl
- Serving bowls
- Juicer
- Cling film

INGREDIENTS

- 350g (12oz) plums, roughly chopped
- 350g (12oz) raspberries
- 2 tsp soft brown sugar
- Juice of 1 lemon

FOR THE TOPPING

- 125g (4½oz) marzipan, grated
- ¼ tsp ground cinnamon

1 Put the fruit in the mixing bowl. Scatter over the sugar and squeeze in the lemon juice.

2 Stir together, then cover with cling film and leave to sit for 1 hour – the sugar and lemon will draw the juices out of the fruit and soften everything up.

3 Sprinkle the marzipan and cinnamon directly into the crumble base from opposite. Once the fruit is ready, divide into 6 bowls, then scatter the crumble topping over the fruit.

Here are 2 more types of
crumble for you to try.
Grab a spoon and dig in!

**25 mins,
plus soaking**

Makes 6

TOOLS

- Sharp knife
- Chopping board
- Spoons
- Scales
- Serving bowls
- Mixing bowl
- Juicer
- Cling film

INGREDIENTS

- 350g (12oz)
  strawberries, halved
- 350g (12oz)
  blueberries
- 2 tsp soft brown sugar
- Juice of 1 lemon

FOR THE TOPPING

- 100g (3½oz) milk
  chocolate chips
- 50g (1¾oz) roasted
  chopped hazelnuts

STRAWBERRY
AND
BLUEBERRY

 1 Pop the strawberries and
blueberries in the mixing bowl,
add the sugar and lemon juice.
Stir together, then cover with cling
film and leave to sit for 1 hour.

 2 Mix the chocolate chips and
hazelnuts into the crumble
base from p. 116. Once the
fruit is ready, divide into 6 bowls,
then add the crumble topping.
Share it with five lucky friends!

25 mins, plus soaking

Makes 6

INGREDIENTS

- 350g (12oz) pineapple chunks
- 350g (12oz) mango chunks
- 2 tsp soft brown sugar
- Juice of 1 lime

FOR THE TOPPING

- 50g (1¾oz) desiccated coconut
- Zest of 1 lime

TOOLS

- Spoons
- Scales
- Serving bowls
- Mixing bowl
- Microplane
- Cling film

TIP

Zest the lime before you juice it – it's much easier to zest a plump, whole lime.

PINEAPPLE AND MANGO

 1 Put the pineapple and mango in the mixing bowl, then sprinkle in the sugar and pour in the lime juice.

 2 Mix well, then cover with cling film and set aside for 1 hour.

 3 Mix the desiccated coconut and lime zest into the crumble base from p. 116. When the fruit has softened, put into 6 bowls, then top with the crumble topping.

 4 Serve with ice cream or custard – coconut ice cream is especially nice!

1 Line the loaf tin with cling film so the sides are covered. You'll need to leave enough cling film hanging over the sides of the tin to cover the top of the semifreddo.

 2 See p. 16 for how to separate egg yolks and whites. Put the yolks into a mixing bowl with the sugar. Using the electric whisk, whip them for 2–3 minutes until the mixture is airy with a pale colour.

 3 Mix in the creamed coconut and most of the lime zest until combined with the egg yolks.

 4 Clean the whisk, then put the cream, yogurt, and lime juice into another mixing bowl. Whip until you have soft peaks. Set aside.

SEMIFREDDOS

A semifreddo is an Italian ice cream cake!
It's super creamy and melts in your mouth.
Turn the page to see more flavours to make.

FOR THE LIME, GINGER, AND COCONUT

- 2 large eggs
- 50g (1¾oz) caster sugar
- 50g (1¾oz) sachet of creamed coconut
- Zest and juice of 2 limes
- 100ml (3½fl oz) double cream
- 100g (3½oz) full-fat Greek yogurt
- 6 ginger biscuits, roughly crushed
- Toasted coconut flakes, to serve

* Please note: the finished recipe contains uncooked egg.

TOOLS

- 450g (1lb) loaf tin
- Cling film
- Scales
- Electric whisk
- Mixing bowls
- Spatula
- Microplane
- Spoons
- Plate
- Measuring jug

30 mins, plus freezing

Serves 6–8

5 Clean the whisk again, then put the egg whites into another mixing bowl. Whisk for 2–3 minutes until stiff peaks form.

6 Use a metal spoon to fold the cream into the egg yolk mixture – be careful not to knock the air out. Fold in one spoonful of the egg whites until everything is mixed.

7 Gently fold in the remaining egg whites – only add a little at a time, until everything is smooth and airy. It will be quite a loose mixture.

8 Carefully fold in most of the crushed biscuits, then spoon the mix into the loaf tin. Cover the top with cling film, then freeze for at least 12 hours, or up to 1 week.

Remove the cling film, then scatter over the remaining crushed biscuits. Sprinkle the rest of the lime zest and coconut flakes on top to decorate.

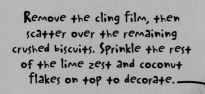

TIP
To make the creamed coconut easy to mix, pop the sachet in warm water for 15–20 minutes.

TO SERVE
Take out of the freezer and leave for 15–20 minutes. Put a plate on top of the tin, then flip them both over together. The semifreddo should fall out – tug the cling film if it doesn't.

FOR THE APRICOT AND PISTACHIO

- 2 large eggs
- 50g (1¾oz) caster sugar
- 1 tsp vanilla extract
- 100ml (3½ floz) double cream
- 100g (3½oz) full-fat Greek yogurt
- 5 tbsp apricot compote, or jam
- 50g (1¾oz) pistachios, roughly crushed
- 1 apricot, sliced, to serve

* Please note: the finished recipe contains uncooked egg.

TOOLS

- 450g (1lb) loaf tin
- Cling film
- Scales
- Electric whisk
- Mixing bowls
- Spatula
- Spoons
- Pestle and mortar
- Metal spoon
- Sharp knife
- Chopping board

30 mins, plus freezing

Serves 6–8

1 Repeat step 1 from p. 120.

4 Fold in the apricot compote or jam and most of the pistachios. Spoon into the loaf tin, then cover with the cling film and freeze.

2 Repeat step 2 from p. 120, but add the vanilla extract.

5 Follow the "To serve" instructions on p. 121.

3 Repeat steps 4–7 from pp. 120–121, but don't add the lime juice in step 4.

6 Remove the cling film, then arrange the apricot slices and the rest of the pistachios on top.

FOR THE ETON MESS

- 2 large eggs
- 50g (1¾oz) caster sugar
- 1 tsp vanilla extract
- 150g (5½oz) strawberries
- 150g (5½oz) raspberries
- 1 tbsp icing sugar
- 100ml (3½fl oz) double cream
- 100g (3½oz) full-fat Greek yogurt
- 8 mini meringues

* Please note: the finished recipe contains uncooked egg.

30 mins, plus freezing

Serves 6–8

The name of this semifreddo comes from a traditional English dessert, made with cream, berries, and meringue.

TOOLS

- 450g (1lb) loaf tin
- Cling film
- Scales
- Electric whisk
- Mixing bowls
- Spatula
- Spoons
- Pestle and mortar
- Metal spoon
- Sharp knife
- Chopping board
- Fork

1 Repeat step 1 from p. 120.

2 Repeat step 2 from p. 120, but add the vanilla extract.

3 Repeat steps 4–7 from pp. 120–121, but don't add the lime juice in step 4.

4 Put 100g (3½oz) each of strawberries and raspberries and the icing sugar into a bowl. Use the fork to roughly crush together.

5 Fold the crushed berries into the semifreddo mixture and crumble in 6 meringues. Spoon into the loaf tin, then cover with the cling film and freeze.

6 Follow the "To serve" instructions on p. 121. Remove the cling film, then crumble over the rest of the meringues and top with the leftover berries.

GLOSSARY

BLEND
Mix ingredients together in a blender or food processor until combined

CHILL
Cool down in the fridge, or keep cool

CHOP
Use a knife to cut ingredients into smaller pieces

CITRUS
Sharp flavour of citrus fruits, such as lemons and limes

COMBINE
Mix ingredients together evenly

CRÊPE
Thin pancake

DICE
Cut ingredients into small, equal cubes

DRAIN
Remove liquid from something and let it flow somewhere else, such as into a sink

DRIZZLE
Pour slowly, in a trickle

FLORET
Small, flower-shaped piece of a vegetable, such as cauliflower

FOLD
Mix ingredients together gently without knocking the air out

GARNISH
Toppings added to a dish before serving

GRATE
Shred ingredients into little pieces by rubbing them against a grater

GRIND
Crush ingredients until they become a fine powder

JUICE
Squeeze the liquid out of fruits or vegetables

MARINATE
Soak food in other ingredients so it can develop a certain flavour

PITTED
Food that has had its stone removed

PORTION
Amount or helping of food

PURÉE
Thick pulp, usually of fruit or vegetables

RINDLESS
Without an outer skin, such as rindless goat's cheese

SEASON
Add salt, pepper, herbs, or spices to food

SLICE
Use a knife to cut food into strips

SUBSTITUTE
Change one ingredient for another

TEXTURE
Way an ingredient feels when you touch or taste it. For example, it could be smooth or rough

THICKEN
When a liquid becomes stiffer and more solid

VARIATION
Another option to prepare the recipe, either with different ingredients or a different way of presenting the dish

WHISK
Evenly mix ingredients together with a whisk or electric whisk

INDEX

ACKNOWLEDGEMENTS

The author would like to thank: Katie Lawrence and the team at DK, for their help and support (especially during the trials of testing during lockdown!); her son Henry who was an incredibly enthusiastic guinea pig, and her husband Oliver for eating uncooked meals every day for a month and being nice about all of them. Also to Jess Meyer — recipe tester and assistant extraordinaire, for taking the time to beautifully style each one of the recipes for the test shots. A simple gesture but very much appreciated!

DK would like to thank: Vanessa Bird for the index; Laura Nickoll for proofreading; Lynne Murray for picture library assistance; James Mitchem for editorial advice; and Anne Damerell for legal assistance.

The publisher would like to thank the following for their kind permission to reproduce their photographs:

(Key: a-above; b-below/bottom; c-centre; f-far; l-left; r-right; t-top)

10 Dreamstime.com: Airborne77 (br); Catherine Eckert (cb); Christophe Testi (cra); Penchan Pumila / Gamjai (cr); Alexander Pladdet / Pincarel (bc/Garbage bag); Anton Starikov (bl, bc, crb). **11 Dreamstime.com:** Airborne77 (bl); AntonStarikov (clb). **15 123RF.com:** Karandaev (crb). **28 Dreamstime.com:** Marian Pentek Digihelion. **29 Dreamstime.com:** Dusan Kostic (cr). **59 Dreamstime.com:** Philip Kinsey (ca). **100-101 Dreamstime.com:** Maljalen (c)

All other images © Dorling Kindersley
For further information see: www.dkimages.com